ISAIAH'S IMMANUEL

A Sign of His Times
Or the Sign of the Ages?

EDWARD E. HINDSON

PRESBYTERIAN AND REFORMED PUBLISHING CO.
PHILLIPSBURG, NEW JERSEY
1979

Copyright 1978
Presbyterian and Reformed Publishing Co.
International Library Series
Robert L. Reymond, *editor*

ISBN: 0-87552-310-2

DEDICATION

TO

DR. EDWARD J. YOUNG

whose devotion to Christ and the Scriptures has done more in the twentieth century than any other single man to advance the study of Isaiah's prophecies.

CONTENTS

ABOUT THE AUTHOR

Dr. Edward E. Hindson is Professor of Religion at Liberty Baptist College, Lynchburg, Virginia. A recognized Old Testament scholar, Dr. Hindson holds earned degrees from five schools: B.A., Detroit Bible College; M.A., Trinity Evangelical Divinity School; Th.M., Grace Theological Seminary; Th.D., Trinity Graduate School of Theology; D.Min., Westminster Theological Seminary. He has also done graduate studies at Eastern Michigan University, the Mennonite Biblical Seminary, and Acadia University (Canada).

Professor Hindson's earlier works include: *The Philistines and the Old Testament* (1971); *Glory in the Church* (1975); *Introduction to Puritan Theology* (1976). He has studied under such outstanding North American evangelical scholars as Gleason Archer, Ph.D.; Kenneth Barker, Ph.D.; Herbert Bess, Ph.D.; John J. Davis, Th.D.; Walter Kaiser, Ph.D.; Allison Trites, Ph.D.; G. Douglas Young, Ph.D.; John Whitcomb, Th.D. In addition to his college responsibilities, Dr. Hindson lectures widely in colleges and churches and also teaches the largest adult Sunday School class in America at the Thomas Road Baptist Church in Lynchburg, Virginia, with an average attendance of over three thousand.

PREFACE

Isaiah stands at the peak of the Old Testament literary genius of the prophets of ancient Israel. His book is the longest of the prophets and looks further into the future than any of its contemporaries. One of the unique features of Isaiah's writing is his "Immanuel Prophecy" (ch. 7-12), which tells of a great coming child ruler who will be King in Israel. The identification of Immanuel has long been debated as many attempts have been made to demonstrate his significance in these passages. Without a doubt, his proper identification centers on the interpretation of Isaiah 7:14, where a virgin is said to conceive this child.

The virgin birth of Christ has always been one of the foundational doctrines of the Christian church. Only in the last two centuries has this doctrine been seriously questioned, as some have suggested that the passage under consideration does not, in fact, proclaim the virgin birth of the Messiah. Are these numerous objections valid, or do they merely represent the same uncritically repeated thoughts of others? Liberal scholarship has attempted to sweep away the textual evidence on this passage, while failing to answer the clear and lucid arguments of such conservative scholars as Edward J. Young. Indeed, it would appear that they have no legitimate answers, since none have effectively replied to Young's arguments.

Historically, the Christian church has interpreted Isaiah 7:14 as a messianic prediction. Only after a barrage of critical attempts to reject that interpretation did evangelicals switch to the so-called "double fulfillment" view of this passage as an attempted compromise between the two positions. Like most compromise views, it created more problems than it solved. Nearly seventy years passed from Orelli's commentary until Young's, in which the compromise position reached its peak. While the question of Immanuel's identification is still debated, more evangelicals than ever are returning to the single fulfillment view of Isaiah 7:14 as a messianic prediction of the virgin birth of Christ.

This present study was originally begun as a Master's thesis at Trinity Evangelical Divinity School, Deerfield, Illinois, ten years ago. Additional research over these years has continued to reconfirm the original research. Isaiah's Immanuel was not just a sign of his times—he was truly THE SIGN OF THE AGES!

Special acknowledgement is due Dr. Norman Geisler, a former instructor who first called my attention to the conflict over the interpretation of this passage, and to Dr. Gleason Archer and Dr. Walter Kaiser, who served on my original thesis committee. Also, a word of sincere appreciation is due Dr. John Whitcomb, another devout evangelical scholar whose lectures on Isaiah were profoundly helpful in my continued study of this matter, as well as the publishers who are committed to the publication of scholarship which honors the inspired Scriptures.

EDWARD E. HINDSON, TH.D.
Liberty Baptist College
Lynchburg, Virginia
January 17, 1978

Chapter One

INTRODUCTION

TEXT

Isaiah 7:10-16[1]

10 And the Lord spake again unto Ahaz saying.

11 Ask for thyself a sign from the Lord God, make deep the request or make it high above.

12 And Ahaz said, I will not ask, and I will not tempt the Lord.

13 And he said, Hear ye now, O house of David; is it too little for you to weary men, that ye weary also my God?

14 Therefore the Lord himself will give you a sign. Behold! a virgin is with child and will bring forth a son and she shall call his name Immanuel.

15 Butter and honey will he eat when he knows to reject the evil and choose the good.

16 For before the child knows to reject the evil and choose the good, the land which thou abhorrest will be forsaken of her two kings.

LIFE AND MINISTRY OF ISAIAH

Isaiah, the son of Amoz, was one of the most prominent citizens of Jerusalem, having access to the royal and priestly leadership of the nation. *Yesha'-Yahu means* "the Lord is salvation."[2] The significance of his name is revealed in his prophetic ministry, for he came upon the scene of Judah's history at a time when it was of the utmost importance for the nation to realize that salvation was from God, not by man's efforts. Many feel this was a pivotal point in the

---

1. Young's translation in *The Book of Isaiah* (Grand Rapids: Eerdmans, 1965), vol. I, pp. 277-78.
2. Ibid. He prefers this rendering to "the salvation of the Lord."

nation's history, when it began to turn from the concept of a theocracy to one of dependence upon and alliance with the surrounding foreign nations. The appearance of the Assyrian nation upon the horizon of Near Eastern politics signaled the beginning of a striving for universalism as nations attempted to establish a world empire. In the face of such opposition stood this man Isaiah, who declared that it was not God's purpose for his people to become engulfed by this growing empire.

Isaiah has been described as the most notable figure after David in the entire history of Israel.[3] In the face of national crises he practically guided the helm of the state in Hezekiah's day, encouraging Jerusalem to hold out against the Assyrian invasion when all others were ready to submit. He has been called "the most powerful statesman in Jerusalem."[4] His main distinction, however, was moral and intellectual rather than political. His influence was of great and lasting effect upon Hebrew polity and religion. His literary efforts may be termed the "classical period" in Hebrew literature. That his book should stand at the head of the seventeen prophetic works is no mistake. Baxter writes that all who have an appreciation for literature must be impressed by Isaiah's combined excellence of style.[5] The grandeur and dignity are paralleled by a liveliness of energy and profusion of imagery. His wide variety is seen in the forcefulness of plays on words, a vividness of description, and dramatic rhetorical touches.

Isaiah's long life spanned the rule of several kings. Born during the reign of Uzziah, Isaiah was called to his prophetic ministry the year that he died (740 B.C.). The prophet's birth, then, was likely to have been c. 770–760 B.C. Jotham came to the throne from 750 to 732 B.C. He was followed by Ahaz (732–715 B.C.), and finally by Hezekiah (c. 716–686 B.C.).[6] In his early years Isaiah saw Judah

---

3. W. R. Smith, *The Prophets of Israel* (New York: Appleton & Co., 1882), p. 208.

4. J. Adams, *The Hebrew Prophets and Their Message for Today* (Edinburgh: T. & T. Clark, 1928), p. 78.

5. J. S. Baxter, *Explore the Book* (Grand Rapids: Zondervan, 1962), p. 217.

6. Of all the dates of the Hebrew kings these are the most unsettled. For the old standard dates see E. Thiele, *The Mysterious Numbers of the Hebrew*

in a time of prosperity and military strength. Soon, however, the rise of Tiglath-pileser III (or Pul) in Assyria became a constant threat to Judah's safety.[7] Rapid change came upon Israel as Menahem died, Pekahiah was murdered, and by 740 B.C. Pekah seized the throne in Samaria. The same year Uzziah died in Judah. Pekah immediately began an aggressive anti-Assyrian policy. At the same time, however, a pro-Assyrian party was gaining influence in Judah. At this juncture, Ahaz came to the throne of Judah.[8] Having rejected the prophet's advice, Ahaz continued the pro-Assyrian policy, and little else is heard of Isaiah during his reign, after the events of chapter 7. With the accession of Hezekiah to the throne a new day came upon Judah. Pursuing a policy of reforms, the new king repaired and cleansed the temple and returned the emphasis to the Mosaic law in determining national ethics. Isaiah became a prime figure during these years as Hezekiah's chief advisor. How long the prophet lived beyond his associations with Hezekiah around 700 B.C., we do not know. Possibly he lived as long as until 680 B.C., when Sennacherib died.[9] Tradition says that he was sawn in half by Manasseh, the evil king who followed Hezekiah.[10]

Not all, however, have held such an esteemed view of the prophet. Many have attempted to relegate his book to the class of a mere

Kings (Grand Rapids: Eerdmans, 1965), pp. 75-98, and F. F. Bruce, *Israel and the Nations* (Grand Rapids: Eerdmans, 1963), p. 229. For the corrected dates see K. Kitchen and T. Mitchell, "Chronology of the Old Testament," in J. Douglas, ed., *New Bible Dictionary* (Grand Rapids: Eerdmans, 1962), p. 217; and H. Stigers, "The Interphased Chronology of Jotham, Ahaz, Hezekiah and Hoshea," *Bulletin of the Evangelical Theological Society* IX, 2 (Spring, 1966). They point out that Thiele's dates for this period are about twelve years off. The problem is caused by overlapping co-regencies when Jotham actually comes to the throne in 750 and shares the rule for ten years. Ahaz also shares a co-regency from c. 744 to 735. Hezekiah then shares a co-regency with Ahaz from c. 729 to 716. Cf. chart in *N.B.D.,* p. 220.

7. S. Schultz, *The Old Testament Speaks* (New York: Harper & Row, 1960), p. 300, indicates that as early as 743 B.C. he exacted tribute from Uzziah of Judah and Menahem of Israel.

8. For a more complete discussion of the historical setting of relations between Ahaz and Isaiah see chapter 3.

9. See discussion in S. Schultz, op. cit., p. 302.

10. See references in Josephus, *Antiquities,* 10:3:1, or Justin Martyr, *Dialogue With Trypho,* 120. Also see the account in the pseudepigraphic book, *The Ascension of Isaiah.* Also notice the reference in Hebrews 11:37 to Old Testament saint(s) being "sawn asunder."

collection of prophetic scribblings, collected and given a "legendary" quality by a later writer. A discreditation of the man and/or his writing has come from many recent writers, who maintain that he was never really able to so distinctly predict future events as his book would indicate.[11] It has become popular to consider prophetic writings as a late collection that was "up-dated" by a redactor.[12] It is quite obvious that one's basic assumptions in regard to the authority of Scripture and the scope of prophecy will determine his interpretation of the content of a given prophetic book.[13] What of this man Isaiah? Was he the authoritative spokesman of God or the invention of literary imagination? It is this writer's view that, as a man of God, Isaiah stood before the political and religious leaders of his day, proclaiming the message of God. His lips moved to proclaim both judgment and blessing. He claimed to be God's spokesman. Who has proven that he was not telling the truth?[14] There is not yet available any evidence to challenge the historicity of the man and his ministry.[15] This prophet, poet, orator, and literary genius

---

11. A Jewish scholar, S. Blank, writes in *Prophetic Faith in Isaiah* (New York: Harper Brothers, 1958), p. 9, "The next 'Isaiah' after the first was no Isaiah at all, because he was no man but only the shadow of a man. . . . The Isaiah of legend, shaped almost wholly by the popular mind, is a barely recognizable shadow of the historical Isaiah. . . . The historical Isaiah was consistent, but he was wrong. As a predictor he had failed and he was discredited . . . yet, he was remembered and as time went on, remembered other than he had been. A later generation credited him at least with the power to forecast more closely the course of events. Hindsight supplied what foresight had not envisaged." One wonders where Blank has obtained his well-verified historical "facts"!

12. For an early representation of this view see W. R. Smith, op. cit., p. 210. He maintains that Isaiah's loose bits of prophecy were pieced together about two hundred-fifty years after his death during the time of Ezra.

13. For an example of one holding Smith's view see S. R. Driver, op. cit., p. 42. He implies that the figure of Immanuel in chapter 7 is an ideal one, projected upon the "shifting future" as the "unpremeditated creation" of Isaiah's own imagination.

14. Jamieson, Fausset, and Brown, *Commentary on the Whole Bible* (Grand Rapids: Zondervan, n.d.), p. 12, gives certain points that were Jewish criteria for discerning a true prophet: (1) The fulfillment of his prophecy. (2) His speaking in the name of *Yahweh*. (3) His accordance of his message to the precepts of the law. (4) His only promising prosperity on the basis of repentance. (5) His own assurance of his divine message. (6) His producing in others that same assurance.

15. The oldest available document is 1QIs[a] (St. Mark's Manuscript) from

still deserves our recognition as an outstanding man of God whose insight of faith produced a greater foresight into the Christological significance of God's plan for His people. Certainly we must agree with the inspired record of the New Testament, which says he "saw Christ's day and spoke of him" (John 12:41).

No man in his own strength could meet the challenge of the day as a prophet sent from God. With the message of God upon his lips, Isaiah was such a man, inspired of God to proclaim a message that needed to be heard.[16] This writer holds that Isaiah himself was the author of his entire book and that he collected and edited his messages into the present composition. The inner unity of the book and the external evidence are most adequate to support this view.[17] The present discussion centers upon the interpretation of Immanuel, and not the evaluation of the unity of the entire book, which is assumed in the following discussion.

LEADING WRITERS

Many men in the past two centuries have written from various viewpoints concerning Isaiah's prophecies. In the next chapter we shall discuss the viewpoints of mainline conservative writers with regard to the Immanuel passage. Now, however, let us consider briefly all the major writers who have lent their efforts to extensive studies of the book of Isaiah.

During the Reformation the outstanding commentators were Luther

the Dead Sea Scrolls collection. It cannot date later than 100 B.C. and is probably older. It gives no indication of the disunity of authorship in the book. See Mansoor, *The Dead Sea Scrolls* (Grand Rapids: Eerdmans, 1964), pp. 69-81, for a good outlined discussion and description of the scroll and its contents.

16. See the excellent discussion of prophets as recipients of revelation in E. Young, *My Servants the Prophets* (Grand Rapids: Eerdmans, 1952), pp. 161-190.

17. The oldest available manuscripts do not show any evidence of disunity between the major sections of the book as claimed by most modern critical writers. Jesus' references to Isaiah as the author of the book are almost equally divided between both "halves" of the so-called Deutero composition. For very thorough treatments of the authorship and unity problems in Isaiah see O. T. Allis, *The Unity of Isaiah* (Philadelphia: Presbyterian and Reformed, 1950), pp. 1-50; G. Archer, *A Survey of Old Testament Introduction* (Chicago: Moody Press, 1964), pp. 314-339; E. Young, *Who Wrote Isaiah?* (Grand Rapids: Eerdmans, 1958).

(1528), Zwingli (1529), and Calvin (1570). Their works reflect a true understanding of prophecy and of the message of the Old Testament. Since their time the main works on Isaiah have appeared during the past two centuries.

Carl R. Reichel (1759) wrote two volumes from an orthodox standpoint, seeking to bring out the true meaning of the prophecy.

John Gill (1771) was a Baptist minister whose extensive works represent a biblical concept of prophecy. His writing is replete with references to rabbinical literature.

Robert Lowth (1778) produced a valuable work with an esthetic and poetic emphasis, quoting often from classical writers. Though denying the unity of authorship, his comments on the Immanuel passage uphold a messianic viewpoint.

J. Michaelis (1778) was the forerunner of the modern criticism that characterized the nineteenth century.

H. E. G. Paulos (1793) reflected a rationalistic concept of prophecy, but is very useful from a philological standpoint.

E. F. Rosenmüller (1791–93) wrote a commentary in Latin that contains valuable philological comments despite its rationalistic basis.

G. L. Bauer (1794) produced a homiletical commentary designed for pastors.

O. Eichhorn (1819) interpreted the prophecy as being contained in poetic descriptions of the present and never as predictive of the future.

W. Gesenius (1821) used many references to the Arabic. His philological notes are excellent, but his view of the prophecy is rather low.

E. Hengstenberg (1829) emphasized the messianic interpretation and has produced a valuable work relating to Isaiah. He is very conservative and very thorough.

A. Barnes (1840) was conservative and very extensive. He held a dual-fulfillment view on most of the messianic prophecies. At times his theological statements lack clear biblical support.

J. Alexander (1846) produced a two-volume work that is one of the best. The discussion of Hebrew forms is very thorough, and the comments are quite extensive and very conservative.

M. Drechsler (1849) has written another of the finest works on the book of Isaiah. His understanding of prophecy is very conservative and very thorough.

E. Meyer (1850) writes mainly from a standpoint of showing the ethical concern of the prophets.

A. Keith (1850) has produced a helpful commentary. However, he is not always clear on the messianic significance of basic passages, and he tends to be quite "wordy."

S. Luzatto (1855) was an Orthodox Jew and expounded the text from that viewpoint, generally deleting any messianic significance.

F. Delitzsch (1866) was very extensive in his philological comments and very orthodox in his beliefs. His work is one of the very finest on Isaiah.

T. K. Cheyne (1868) was also thorough and his book, which is far more conservative than his later writings, is quite helpful.

H. Cowles (1869) is a very fine work on Isaiah. He deals with all the problem sections, and is especially thorough on the Immanuel section.

T. Birks (1878) is very conservative and gives a good exposition of the book. He has an extensive section on messianic prophecy.

S. R. Driver (1888) actually wrote of the man Isaiah in a series on great men in the Bible. Yet, this volume is crammed full of his higher critical viewpoints on Isaian authorship.

G. A. Smith (1888) wrote two volumes in popular-lecture style. However, they reflect a low view of prophecy and the prophetic mission.

B. Duhm (1892) suggested a trito-Isaiah view of the authorship. He was quite radical and free with textual emendations. Also, he was very influential.

C. Von Orelli (1895) does not defend the unity of authorship by Isaiah, but his views are generally very high and conservative. He accepts the messianic prophecies and in general has produced a fine commentary.

J. Skinner (1896) provides helpful introductory material and extensive notes. His work, however, is generally a repetition of Duhm.

G. L. Robinson (1912) produced a brief outline study of the book which is most helpful as a study guideline. It is conservative and still in print.

G. B. Gray (1912) wrote a philologically excellent work for the

International Critical Commentary series. It has long been the standard work on Isaiah, but it has mainly a rationalistic basis and denies the messianic significance of prophecy.

J. Ridderbos (1922) wrote a commentary in Dutch that represents the Reformed position.

F. Feldman (1924) was a Catholic who attempted to return to a sober exegesis of the book.

C. Boutflower (1930) was a critical interpreter with some very radical views.

J. Fischer (1937) is also a Catholic and less conservative than Feldman, but his comments on the Servant passages are very good.

E. J. Kissane (1941) is also a Roman Catholic, but is much freer with textual emendations and critical comments. His arguments in relation to the Immanual passage are brief and generally unfounded.

A. Bentzen (1944) wrote in Danish and covered the prophecy from modern Scandinavian viewpoint, reflecting the influence of Mowinckel.

B. Copass (1944) is a Southern Baptist writer and has produced a helpful work for the English reader. He is theologically conservative and upholds the messianic interpretation of prophecy.

W. Kelley (1947) is very devotional and does not deal with technical problems. His position, though, is very conservative.

F. C. Jennings (1950) is Brethren and conservative. His work is more expositional than exegetical but is a very fine study. He holds a double-fulfillment view of the Immanuel passage.

W. E. Vine (1953) is an Englishman. His book is actually more of a "study" than a commentary. His theology is conservative, and his approach is very helpful. He usually deals with the important "problem" sections.

C. R. Erdman (1954) has written a brief study of the book of Isaiah. It is conservative, messianic, and concise.

J. Steinman (1955) has also done a study of the prophecy from a Catholic standpoint. He is quite conservative and is sometimes helpful.

Interpreter's Bible (1956) covers the entire prophecy with exegetical and expositional comments. It assumes the multiple authorship of the prophecy. The exegetical comments usually deny any messianic implications in the prophecies, while the expositor usually accepts them!

S. Blank (1958) is a Jewish writer who has taken an extremely radical position toward the book. He is extremely free with textual emendations and does not regard the historical Isaiah as having been at all important in the affairs of Judah.

P. Schilling (1958) has written to popularize the "three Isaiah" theory. He is not very extensive in his treatment of the problems.

A. Penna (1958) has written a very helpful book in Italian. His comments are extensive, and his historical background is very helpful.

J. Muckle (1960) produced a homiletical commentary on Isaiah that is brief and generally critical of the messianic passages.

J. Mauchline (1962) is Neo-Orthodox and denies the messianic implication of most of the prophecies. His study of the book is helpful though. He is a good "standard" representative of many contemporary writers.

E. Leslie (1963) is a Methodist. His work is a conglomeration of exegesis, homiletical abstracts, outline studies, *et al.* Most of his comments are quite shallow in dealing with the main areas of the prophecy.

E. Young (1965–72) has produced a three-volume commentary that is the best thing written on Isaiah in over a century. He is conservative and sees the significance of the messianic prophecies. His discussion of philological matters is extensive and lends excellent support to his viewpoints. This set will certainly become a "standard" conservative work for many years to come. Dr. Young died in 1969, after completing the second volume. The third volume was published posthumously in 1972, from his earlier preparations.

J. Ward (1969) produced a typical modern commentary in which he attempted to avoid committing himself to any specific views.

O. Kaiser (1972) began a critical commentary on the early chapters of Isaiah but died before covering the entire book.

MESSIANIC PROPHECY

Before proceeding to the main discussion of Isaiah's Immanuel, a brief examination of the message and method of messianic prophecy should be considered.

The Prophet and the Prophetic Ministry

The prophetical histories are followed in the Hebrew canon by the prophetical books of prediction. The two form a unit in the middle portion of the threefold canon, under the common term נְבִיאִים ("prophets"). They are distinguished as the נְבִיאִים הָרִאשֹׁנִים ("former prophets") and הָאַחֲרוֹנִים ("latter prophets").[18]

The usage of נָבִיא designates the prophet as a spokesman for God.[19] Though often radical in his approach, the nineteenth-century Dutch theologian Kuenen, of the University of Leyden, rightly asked for a re-examination of the office and work of the prophet because of the orthodox over-emphasis upon the merely predictive aspect of prophecy.[20] However, this does not allow the opposite extreme to throw out all predictive aspects of prophecy.[21] It is true that prophecy has its roots in history.[22] It also, however, has a definite reference to the future in some cases, and that reference is taken from the writer's historical standpoint. So that the prophet does speak primarily to men of his own time, and his message springs out of the circumstances in which he lives. Yet for all this, the source of that message is supernatural, not natural. Ellison writes:

> It is derived neither from observation nor intellectual thought, but from admission to the council chamber of God, from knowing God and speaking with Him.[23]

Thompson traces this concept in the Old Testament, noting that the prophet is admitted to God's council chamber, where God "re-

---

18. For a very thorough discussion of the relationship of the historical and predictive prophecies see F. Delitzsch, *Biblical Commentary on the Prophecies of Isaiah* (Grand Rapids: Eerdmans, 1949), vol. I, pp. 1-27.

19. See its early usage in Exodus 4:15, 16. Moses is as God in relation to the pharaoh, and Aaron is his "spokesman."

20. Kuenen, op. cit., pp. 1-16.

21. See Driver, op. cit., pp. 3ff., for a representative of this viewpoint. He maintains that the prophets always address themselves to the present and never predict the future.

22. A. B. Davidson, *Old Testament Prophecy* (Edinburgh: T. & T. Clark, 1903), pp. 247-68, had a great influence in spreading this concept of prophecy. However, he limited prophecy to only the historical aspect and saw Isaiah as merely looking back over historical events as he wrote. For a good criticism of his methods see Allis, op. cit., pp. 127-28.

23. H. L. Ellison, *Men Spake From God* (Grand Rapids: Eerdmans, 1952), p. 14.

veals his secrets" (Amos 3:7). "Reveal" (גָּלָה) means "uncover" (I Sam. 9:15—"uncovering of the ear"). He concludes that when God "uncovers" the prophet's ear, He reveals what is hidden (II Sam. 7:27), so that the prophet in turn "perceives" and "gives heed to" what the Lord said (Jer. 23:18).[24]

It is obvious, therefore, that the "Spirit of God" is necessary for prophetic inspiration (Isa. 30:1ff.). Thus, it was by the Spirit that the Word of the Lord was communicated to the prophet and by the Spirit that the Word was mediated to the people.[25] This communion with God was indispensable to the prophetic consciousness as a medium of revelation, so that under the guidance of the Holy Spirit prophecy can sometimes be quite startling in the individuality and definiteness of its prediction of even remote events.[26] So we see the full picture of prophecy as both a forthtelling of God's messages and a foretelling of God's actions. Through this means God continued to energize the prophet to speak for Him.[27] Isaiah was such a man, addressing himself to his own times as he brought God's direction to the kings of Judah and also a man seeing far into the future of God's plans for His people.

The Messiah in Prophecy

The high aspirations of the Old Testament writers and their ascriptions of God-like characteristics to a coming Prince, the Messiah, the Son of David, compel the reader to see one who is more than a mere man. Early he was called both the son of David and the son of God.[28] Girdlestone pointed out that there is no definite statement that all these references in the Old Testament are to be fulfilled in

---

24. J. G. Thomson, *The Old Testament View of Revelation* (Grand Rapids: Eerdmans, 1960), p. 40.

25. Ibid., p. 41.

26. Discussed by J. Orr, *The Problem of the Old Testament* (New York: Scribner's Sons, 1907), pp. 461ff.

27. In speaking of the importance of the doctrine of inspiration Young, *Thy Word Is Truth* (Grand Rapids: Eerdmans, 1957), p. 191, warns: "If we reject this foundational supposition of Christianity we shall arrive at results which are hostile to supernatural Christianity. . . . If one begins with man he will end with man. If one begins with the presuppositions of unbelief he will end with unbelief's conclusions."

28. See comments and passages listed by D. Baron, *Rays of Messiah's Glory* (Grand Rapids: Zondervan, n.d.), p. 37.

one person, but such is the natural conclusion at which the recipients of the Old Testament arrived.[29] Yet with the development of this messianic expectation came the frustrating close of the Old Testament canon, yet awaiting the reality of these hopes embodied in one man.[30] Even Riehm realized that the New Testament based its entire "apologetic " on the basis that Jesus was the Messiah of the Old Testament, and that these are definite predictions which were conclusively fulfilled in this life.[31] Jesus Himself was always aware of the "limitations" prophecy made on Him, since it "must be fulfilled." He subjected Himself completely to the course that they had, under God's direction, prescribed to Him and considered the details of His life and death as something that must take place because it was written in the Word of God. At the same time He saw Himself as the culminating point to which the whole of prophecy pointed.[32]

The purpose of messianic prophecy was to make the Messiah known after He had fulfilled the event foretold. It serves as a preparatory device to signal His arrival.[33] How that "fulfillment" is recognized has been the source of ominous discussion. Alexander warns that although a double-sense of fulfillment is not impossible, it is unreasonable to assume it when any other explanation is admissible. He maintains that it is unlikely that both a common, natural event and a supernatural one would be couched in the same passage.[34] Kraeling refers to three types of prophetic fulfillment in relation to the Messiah ("salutary," "ominous," or both).[35] Sauer also grapples

29. R. Girdlestone, *Old Testament Theology* (London: Longmans, Green and Co., 1909), p. 120.

30. Our point may be well illustrated by a study of the apocryphal apocalyptic books in which that expectation grows intense and distorted. Writers such as Bultmann, *Primitive Christianity in Its Contemporary Setting* (Cleveland: World, 1956), pp. 81-85, try to dissociate the human figure who will restore the Davidic dynasty from the supernatural agent who will provide redemption. To prove this, he quotes from the apocryphal books, but makes no reference at all to the Old Testament teaching itself.

31. E. Riehm, *Messianic Prophecy* (Edinburgh: T. & T. Clark, 1900), p. 216.

32. See the detailed discussion of these concepts in Orelli, *The Prophecies of Isaiah* (Edinburgh: T. & T. Clark, 1895), p. 58.

33. See Hengstenberg, *Christology*, vol. IV, p. 238.

34. J. Alexander, *The Earlier Prophecies of Isaiah* (New York and London: Wiley & Putnam, 1846), p. 170.

35. Kraeling, "The Immanuel Prophecy," in *Journal of Biblical Literature* L (1931): 281.

with three types (direct, typical, and applicable).[36] We must be careful not to look for a "fulfillment" where none is intended or needed to complete the thought of the passage. "Fulfillment" is the consummation of a given prediction in history. The New Testament provides the best guideline to determining whether or not a certain event is fulfilled. It tells us where the prophets spoke of Christ. The indication we are given by the New Testament is that the Old Testament messianic references are a whole that refer totally to one Person, Jesus of Nazareth.

Predictive Nature of Messianic Prophecy

It is difficult to consider the concept of messianic prophecy without assuming some type of "prediction" involved. In this discussion the word *predict* has been used in the ordinary sense of "foretell." The use of the Greek prefix *pro* indicates both "for" and "before." The prophets tell "for" God, and he tells "before" events that will happen. This usage is certified by the parallel synonymity given to "foretell" and "foresee" in the New Testament. Peter, in Acts 2:30ff., speaks of David as a "prophet" because of his "foreseeing" (*proidon*) the resurrection of Christ. It would be ridiculous to insist that this be translated "forthseeing." We can see, then, that the prophets were not always restricted to a "local" sense.[37]

Dr. Culver gives two essential characteristics of predictive prophecy: it must predict the future as only God could know it and bring it to pass, and it must contain a degree of obscurity.[38] This quality of obscurity necessitates a direct fulfillment. It is only when the prophecy has become history that one may reflect upon it to realize

---

36. A. Sauer, "Problems of Messianic Interpretation," in *Concordia Theological Monthly* (October, 1964):566-74. He classifies Isaiah 7:14 as "typical."

37. See Allis, op. cit., pp. 126-27, for a defense of this concept. He states, "This attempt of the critics to eliminate the idea of foretelling from the word 'prophet' indicates very clearly how adverse they are to the admission that foretelling was an important element in prophecy.

38. R. Culver, "Were the Old Testament Prophecies Really Prophetic?" in *Can I Trust My Bible?* (Chicago: Moody Press, 1963), p. 99. His discussion of the significance of the quality of "obscurity" in predictive prophecy is the best I have seen.

that it has been fulfilled.[39] Seen dimly at first, the intent of a prophecy becomes clear with its fulfillment.

The New Testament recognizes the value of predictive prophecy and its fulfillment in using it as apologetical evidence to prove the supernaturalness and credibility of Christianity. In the following discussion Isaiah's prophecy will be thoroughly examined to determine if it is predictive and if so what fulfillment was recognized of it. As a prophet, Isaiah is no mere man; he is a man through whom God communicates the truth. When we determine what he has said, we must recognize it as the truth of God.

---

39. For a good example from the Old Testament see Ezekiel 38:16-17, where God says that long afterwards, when this prophecy was fulfilled, people will remember what the prophets had said and that this event had been predicted beforehand. The fulfillment will bring the remembrance and realization that it has indeed been a fulfillment.

Chapter Two

HISTORICAL DEVELOPMENT OF THE INTERPRETATION
OF ISAIAH SEVEN

In the interpretation of Isaiah seven, three basic positions historically have been taken by commentators: (1) That the reference is
only to an immediate event of the prophet's own day. (2) That it is
only of the Messiah. (3) That it refers to both. The first position
has been generally held by those who have denied the unity of the
book's structure and supernaturalness of the content.[1] There have,
though, been exceptions such as Orelli, who denied the unity of the
book but firmly believed in its supernatural aspects and held the
direct messianic interpretation of 7:14.[2] From the time of the
Reformers most evangelicals held the second viewpoint. Calvin
early reflected this view, maintaining the Christological interpretation of Isaiah seven.[3] Early writers like Bishop Lowth and the Baptist minister, John Gill, also held the messianic interpretation of this
passage.[4] However, during the middle of the nineteenth century, especially after the publication of Duhm's work, the concept of immediate contemporary fulfillment of all of Isaiah's prophecies became

---

1. See such examples as S. R. Driver, *Isaiah: His Life and Times* (London:
Nisbet and Co., 1888); Gray, *The Book of Isaiah* (New York: Scribner's Sons,
1912), vol. I; Duhm, *Das Buch Jesaia* (Gottingen, 1922); Boutflower, *The
Book of Isaiah* (London: SPCK, 1930); Mowinckle, *He That Cometh* (New
York: Abingdon, 1954); Mauchline, *Isaiah 1–39* (New York: Macmillan,
1962); Leslie, *Isaiah* (New York: Abingdon, 1963); G. Knight, *A Christian
Theology of the Old Testament* (London: SCM, 1964).

2. C. Van Orelli, *The Prophecies of Isaiah* (Edinburgh: T. & T. Clark,
1895).

3. See Calvin's position in *Commentary on the Book of Isaiah* (Grand
Rapids: Eerdmans, 1953), p. 246.

4. Lowth, *Isaiah* (Boston: Buckingham, 1815—originally published in 1778),
and Gill, *Body of Divinity* (Grand Rapids: Zondervan, 1951—reprint of 1771
edition).

widespread.[5] Unable to stem the rising flood of opinion, many conservatives retreated to a dual-fulfillment position, especially on this particular passage.[6] Thus, the position of the Reformers, who saw fulfillment only in Christ, was abandoned. This influence affected the interpretation of the entire Immanuel passage, and came to be viewed by many as merely symbolic.[7]

Barnes represents this viewpoint in advocating that "some young female" would bear a son whose name would indicate God's blessing and deliverance. He maintains that only in this way could there have been any satisfactory and convincing evidence to Ahaz. However, he continues that though this is the obvious meaning, there is no doubt that the language is so "couched" as to contain application to a more significant event that was a sign of God's protection. He concludes that "the language, therefore, has at the commencement of the prophecy, a fullness of meaning which is not entirely met by the immediate event."[8]

Beecher also accepted this viewpoint in asserting that the first event of the prediction inadequately fulfills it, but that it is completely fulfilled in a series of events that lead to final culmination.[9]

This concept was historically paralleled by the conservative thinking that the prophet did not know the implication of what he wrote and that his prophecy had "room for" a fuller application. Ellicott represents this concept in maintaining that in the New Testament times the prophecies were seen to have been fulfilled by events in Christ's life even though that meaning was not present to the prophet's own mind.[10]

A contemporary of these men was Dewart, who criticized the

---

5. Duhm, op. cit. For a good discussion of Duhm's methods and the influence he exerted upon other writers see Young, *Studies*, pp. 39-47.

6. Discussed by H. Ellison, *Men Spake From God* (Grand Rapids: Eerdmans, n.d.), p. 14.

7. A. B. Davidson, *Old Testament Prophecy* (Edinburgh: T. & T. Clark, n.d.), p. 268.

8. A. Barnes, *Notes on the Old Testament—Isaiah* (Grand Rapids: Baker, n.d.), vol. I, p. 158.

9. W. Beecher, *The Prophets and the Promise* (Grand Rapids: Baker, n.d.), p. 130.

10. C. Ellicott, *Bible Commentary for English Readers* (London: Cassell & Co., n.d.), p. 438.

views of leading liberals and the condescension of fellow conservatives such as Barnes, Fairbairn, and Riehm.[11] He argues that the true picture of the prophet is given in the Epistles of Peter, who tells us that they did know what they were writing of when they wrote. He challenges conservative writers to evaluate the implications of advocating that the prophets did not know the true meaning of what they wrote. He asks what this does to our concept of inspiration in bending it toward a dictation concept. His book provides several excellent discussions on key passages and is very helpful, though it is very little known today.[12]

The Dutch theologian, Gustav Oehler, also criticized the concept of "double-fulfillment" in the Isaiah seven passage. He felt that the whole context of chapters seven to nine clearly intends a direct messianic interpretation. He admits, ". . . the interpretation now prevailing regards it as only typically Messianic."[13]

His view was followed by Briggs, who also criticized seeing a double-fulfillment in the Isaiah passage. He maintained that a "typical correspondence" is not a direct prediction, for if it can have a "multiple fulfillment," then it was never really a prediction as Matthew obviously regarded it.[14] He sees the sign presented to Ahaz as assigned to the future and, therefore, no immediate fulfillment was to be seen by either Ahaz or Isaiah.[15]

Hengstenberg also maintained that the Christian church had, from the time of the Church Fathers, upheld the direct messianic explanation of Isaiah 7:14. He states that it was not until the mid-eighteenth century that writers began to turn from this view. He

---

11. See the excellent discussion on the viewpoints of his contemporary writers on Isaiah 7:14. He mentions Riehm, Orelli, Oehler, Green, G. A. Smith, Gloay, Davidson, and Cheyne. Dewart, *Jesus the Messiah in Prophecy and Fulfillment* (Cincinnati: Cranston & Stowe, 1891), pp. 128-29.

12. Ibid., pp. 64-73. He provides an excellent criticism of the radical viewpoints of Workman, who advocated the view that there is nothing in the Old Testament that refers to Christ.

13. G. Oehler, *Theology of the Old Testament* (New York: Funk & Wagnalls, 1883; reprint Grand Rapids: Zondervan, n.d.), p. 527.

14. C. Briggs, *Messianic Prophecy* (New York: Scribner's Sons, 1892), pp. 197ff.

15. Ibid., p. 197.

admits that by the mid-nineteenth century it had gained to the point of prevailing over the historic interpretation.[16]

Cowles also criticized the growing double-fulfillment influence upon conservative writers. He gives a thorough discussion of the problems created by the double-fulfillment interpretation of Isaiah 7:14. He concluded that a dual-fulfillment view of the prophecy is really a "single-fulfillment" view in that only the first event is really predicted and the latter one is merely an "analogy."[17] He asks some searching questions, such as why did not the prophet structure the passage to "allow" a multiple meaning? He stresses that the use of the definite article and the verb tenses imply that the prophet has only one person in mind.[18]

Many exegetical writers such as Joseph Alexander and Franz Delitzsch stood for the "single-fulfillment" view of this passage.[19] However, most of the conservatives' homiletical commentaries adopted the dual-fulfillment view and thus it came into the American pulpits.[20]

---

16. Hengstenberg, *A Christology of the Old Testament and a Commentary on Messianic Predictions* (Grand Rapids: Kregal, 1956; reprint of 1829 ed.), vol. III, p. 48. Perhaps the reason Dewart's fine work has become almost unknown is because of Hengstenberg's poor footnotes and mispagination of his writing. Nevertheless, Hengstenberg's volumes are excellent and his notes are very useful.

17. Cowles, *Isaiah: With Notes* (New York: Appleton & Co., 1869), p. 53. This is also a very fine work that has generally been overlooked by most writers.

18. Ibid., p. 54.

19. Alexander, *The Earlier Prophecies of Isaiah* (New York and London: Wiley & Putnam, 1846), pp. 111-114; and Delitzsch, *Biblical Commentary on the Old Testament: Isaiah* (Grand Rapids: Eerdmans, 1949; reprint of 1877 ed.), vol. I, pp. 216-21.

20. See the comments of A. MacClaren, *Expositions of Holy Scripture: Matthew I-VIII* (New York: Hodder and Stoughton, 1906), pp. 10-11. In his commentary on Isaiah he completely skips over the 7:14 passage! In his reference to Matthew 1:23 he accepts the dual-fulfillment position. He states, "The fulfillment does not depend on the question whether or not the idea of virginity is contained in the Hebrew word, but on the correspondence between the figure of the prophet . . . and the person in the gospel." For a criticism of the concept that prophetic fulfillment is merely a "correspondence" see E. J. Young, "Prophets," in *Zondervan Pictorial Bible Dictionary,* ed. M. Tenney (Grand Rapids: Zondervan, 1963), p. 689. He warns, "We must guard against the view that there is merely a correspondence between what the

Many contemporary conservative writers have continued the influence of the multiple-fulfillment interpretation of Isaiah 7:14. These, however, are generally represented in shorter commentaries and journal articles, since there have been no recent conservative commentaries of length on Isaiah except the appearance of Dr. Edward Young's work.[21] Writers such as W. Mueller have advocated that we should accept the RSV translation of *'almah* as "maiden" and use it as an acceptable working basis to present a further correspondence in the passage to the life of Jesus.[22] In his book on hermeneutics, Berkhof discusses the concept of successive fulfillment in prophecy and indicates that he leans toward a double-fulfillment view of this passage.[23] Writing very excellent books on the Gospel of Matthew, H. N. Ridderbos and R. V. G. Tasker also indicate, while commenting on Matthew 1:23, that they see a multiple-fulfillment in the Isaiah 7:14 passage.[24] The fine conservative German writer, Erich Sauer, also indicates that he accepts the concept of double-fulfillment when the appearance of a "type" fulfills part of the prediction and when "this type is also fulfilled in the Messianic development."[25] The only recent extensive conservative commentary

---

prophets say and what occurred in the life of Jesus Christ. There was of course a correspondence, but to say no more than this is not to do justice to the situation. Jesus Christ did not merely find a correspondence between the utterances of the prophets and the events of His own life. . . . So we may say of the entire prophetic body, they saw Christ's day and spoke of Him."

21. Young, *The Book of Isaiah,* in New International Commentary Series (Grand Rapids: Eerdmans, 1965).

22. W. Mueller, "A Virgin Shall Conceive," *Evangelical Quarterly* XXXII, 4 (October, 1960): 203-207. For a good criticism of this viewpoint see the article by W. Robinson, "A Re-Study of the Virgin Birth of Christ," *Evangelical Quarterly* XXXVII, 4 (October, 1965): 198-211, and C. Feinberg, "Virgin Birth in the Old Testament and Isaiah 7:14," *Bibliotheca Sacra* 119 (July, 1962): 251-58.

23. L. Berkhof, *Principles of Biblical Interpretation* (Grand Rapids: Baker, 1950), pp. 137-38.

24. H. Ridderbos, *Matthew's Witness to Jesus Christ* (New York: Association Press, 1958), p. 21, and Tasker, *Gospel According to St. Matthew* (Grand Rapids: Eerdmans, 1961), p. 34. Tasker sees the original intention of the prophecy as signifying the birth of Hezekiah. He maintains that it is Matthew's indication that Isaiah was not really fully aware of the far-reaching consequences of his own prophecy.

25. Sauer, *Dawn of World Redemption* (Grand Rapids: Eerdmans, 1951), pp. 146-47. He classifies all predictions that dealt with events in the gospels

on Isaiah that holds a dual-fulfillment view of Isaiah 7:14 is the work by the Plymouth Brethren writer, F. C. Jennings, who maintains that Immanuel is the prophet's son. He adds this alone, however, cannot fulfill verses 14-15.[26] Since then two major one-volume conservative commentaries have been published that represent a dual-fulfillment view of the Isaiah 7:14 passage.[27] Being very fine works representative of the best British and American evangelical scholarship, they are certain to continue influencing dual-fulfillment interpretation for many years to come. Fitch (*N.B.C.*) sees both an immediate and ultimate fulfillment in the Immanuel passage. He emphasizes that we cannot separate the passage from its messianic emphasis.[28] Dr. Archer (*W.B.C.*) presents an interesting case for viewing the prophet's wife as being typical of the virgin Mary. He relates the fulfillment both to the prophet's son and ultimately to Christ.[29]

Among the recent critics of the dual-fulfillment concept of prophecy the most outspoken have been Barton Payne of Wheaton College and Bernard Ramm of California Baptist Theological Seminary. Payne criticizes Fairbairn's "overdone" typology, which he refers to as a "modified form of dual-fulfillment."[30] He states that if one read only the New Testament, it would be safe to say that he would never suspect the possibility of dual-fulfillment, because the New Testament

and the church age as "spiritually and typically" predictive. This seems to indicate that he does not see a passage like Isaiah 7:14 as directly predictive of Christ. He also lists on pp. 161-62 events relating to the work of the Messiah, beginning with his "birth in Bethlehem" (Mic. 5:2), but he makes no reference at all to Isaiah 7:14; therefore, it is difficult to determine his position on that passage, but his leaving it out indicates that he probably does not consider it directly messianic. For a criticism of Sauer's view of predictive prophecy see B. Payne, "So-Called Dual Fulfillment in Messianic Psalms," in *Printed Papers of the Evangelical Theological Society* (1953 meeting at Chicago), pp. 62-72.

26. Jennings, *Studies in Isaiah* (New York: Loizeau Brothers, 1950), pp. 84-85. He argues that Isaiah's sons are referred to as "signs" in chapter 8 and, therefore, Immanuel must be either Maher-shalal-hash-baz or a third (unknown) son. This is the same position taken exactly a century earlier by A. Keith, *Isaiah As It Is* (Edinburgh: Whyte & Co., 1850), pp. 67-69.

27. F. Davidson, ed., *The New Bible Commentary* (Grand Rapids: Eerdmans, 1954); and C. Pfeiffer and E. Harrison, *The Wycliffe Bible Commentary* (Chicago: Moody Press, 1962).

28. W. Fitch, "Isaiah," in *N.B.C.*, p. 569.

29. G. Archer, "Isaiah," in *W.B.C.*, p. 618.

30. Payne, op. cit., p. 64.

indicates that the predictions refer directly to Christ.[31] Ramm warns that "one of the most persistent hermeneutical sins" is attempting to place two interpretations on one passage of Scripture, thereby breaking the force of the literal meaning and obscuring the picture intended.[32] He concludes that if prophecies have many meanings, then "hermeneutics would be indeterminate."[33]

Workman was the first to categorize the three viewpoints on this passage as: (1) Referring to Christ, (2) not referring to Christ, (3) referring both to a contemporary event and to Christ.[34] The main arguments for each position have been:

Reference to an immediate event:

1. The inquiry involved was not to their final safety but to their present distress.[35]
2. Isaiah's sons' names were a "sign" to the people of his time, and "Immanuel" is a name also directed to his time.[36]
3. The close relation of 8:1-4 indicates that Maher-shalal-hash-baz may well be Immanuel. Even if he were not regularly called Immanuel, remember, neither was "Jesus" so called.[37]
4. The context indicates that the child was to be born before the land was to be forsaken of the two kings from the north.[38]

Reference to the Messiah:

1. Matthew (1:23) regards Jesus as the complete fulfillment of the prophecy.[39]
2. This has been the common (traditional) interpretation of the Christian church.[40]
3. The depth of meaning in the "sign" signifies that permanent destruction cannot come to the land until the Messiah comes

31. Ibid., p. 65.
32. Ramm, *Protestant Biblical Interpretation* (Boston: Wilde, 1956), p. 87.
33. Ibid., p. 88.
34. Cited by Dewart, op. cit., pp. 119-20.
35. Driver, op. cit., p. 40.
36. G. A. Smith, *The Book of Isaiah* (New York: Harper & Brothers, n.d.), vol. I, p. 131.
37. See Gesenius' viewpoint in *Der Prophet Jesaiah* (Leipzig, 1820), pp. 120ff.
38. Barnes, op. cit., p. 140ff.
39. Ridderbos, op. cit., p. 21.
40. Orelli, op. cit., p. 56.

(or he would have nothing to come to). He comes, then, to preserve the remnant.[41]

4. Isaiah's contemporary, Micah, quotes this passage in regard to the birth of the Messiah.[42]

5. The conclusion of this prophetic section in chapters 8–9 is evidently connected to chapter 7.[43]

Reference both to immediate event and to Messiah:

1. Basically this viewpoint accepts the arguments for immediacy of fulfillment in a contemporary event.[44]

2. Also, however, this view is not willing to completely disregard any fulfillment in Christ, so it is generally claimed that Matthew gives us a further development of the Christological aspect involved.[45]

It may be noted from the chart on the following page that as the non-messianic interpretation gained impetus in Germany and began to influence writers in England and the United States during the last half of the nineteenth century, conservative writers of the early twentieth century began to adopt the position earlier advocated by Barnes and Keith.[46] At the same time there was a noticeable drop in commentaries advocating a strictly messianic fulfillment. Meanwhile, the critical viewpoint continued to gain acceptance, especially with the publication of Gray's work as part of the *International Critical Commentary Series*.[47] Such interpretation has a firm foothold today in liberal and neo-orthodox circles. Most of the conservative works advocating single-fulfillment since Orelli were study guides and devotional commentaries, so that Young was right when he wrote in 1954 that "since 1900 no truly great commentaries upon Isaiah have been written."[48] He declared that a great twentieth-century commentary must be written to break with the influence of Duhm.[49] He called for the writing of a new commentary.[50] Eleven years later he answered his own call with the

---

41. Ibid., pp. 56-57.

42. Cowles, op. cit., p. 55.   44. Barnes, op. cit., pp. 140ff.

43. Smith, op. cit., p. 131.   45. MacClaren, op. cit., p. 11.

46. There is a good reason to doubt whether Keith can actually be considered a "conservative."

47. Gray, *The Book of Isaiah* (New York: Scribner's Sons, 1912).

48. Young, *Studies in Isaiah* (Grand Rapids: Eerdmans, 1954), p. 72.

49. Ibid., p. 72.

50. Ibid., p. 100.

Recent English Language Commentaries on Isaiah
And Their View of Isaiah 7:14

MESSIANIC	NON-MESSIANIC	DUAL-FULFILLMENT
Henry (1712)		
Lowth (1778)	Michaelis (1778)	
Clark (1823)		
Hengstenberg (1829)		
Alexander (1846)		Barnes (1840)
Simeon (1847)	Meyer (1850)	Keith (1850)
	Luzzatto (1855)	
Delitzsch (1866)		
Cheyne (1868)		
Cowles (1869)		
Birks (1878)	Ewald (1876)	
	Driver (1888)	
Kay (1886)	Smith (1888)	
Dewart (1891)	Sayce (1889)	Skinner (1896)
Orelli (1895)	Oesterley (1900)	MacClaren (1906)
Robinson (1910)	Gordon (1909)	Naegelsbach (1906)
Gabelein (1912)	Gray (1912)	Plumptre (1920)
Rawlinson (1913)		Exell (1925)
	Torrey (1928)	Williams (1926)
Rogers (1929)	Wade (1929)	
	Boutflower (1930)	
Copass (1944)	Kissane (1941)	
Kelly (1947)		Aberly (1948)
		Jennings (1950)
Vine (1953)		Fitch (1954)
	Interpreter's	
	Bible (1956)	
	Blank (1958)	
	Shilling (1958)	
	Mauchline (1962)	Archer (1962)
Young (1965)	Leslie (1965)	
	Ward (1969)	
	Kaiser (1972)	

publication of volume one of such a commentary.[51] It is a defense of the unity of the book's authorship and of the messianic interpretation of the Immanuel passage. Without a doubt, Young's work on Isaiah is the finest defense of the supernatural-predictive nature of these prophecies available today.[52] We shall be indebted to his work for many years to come.

---

51. In 1965 Eerdmans of Grand Rapids published volume one of an eventual three-volume commentary on Isaiah by E. Young, entitled *The Book of Isaiah.* It was the initial volume of the *New International Commentary* series on the Old Testament. Much of its contents were a compilation of Dr. Young's earlier works: *Studies in Isaiah* (1954); *Who Wrote Isaiah?* (1958); and the appendix material in the revised edition of R. D. Wilson's *A Scientific Investigation of the Old Testament* (Chicago: Moody Press, 1959).

52. Contemporary evangelical scholars have readily acknowledged their dependence upon Young—e.g., cf. R. Gromacki, *The Virgin Birth: Doctrine of Deity* (New York: Thomas Nelson, 1974), p. 144; E. Hindson, "Development of the Interpretation of Isaiah 7:14," *Grace Journal* X (Spring, 1969): 19-25; "Isaiah's Immanuel," *Grace Journal* X (Fall, 1969): 3-15; H. Lindsell, *The Battle for the Bible* (Grand Rapids: Zondervan, 1976), p. 64; R. C. Sproul, "The Case for Inerrence: A Methodological Analysis," in J. W. Montgomery, ed., *God's Inerrant Word* (Minneapolis: Bethany Fellowship, 1974), p. 258.

Chapter Three

MAIN ISSUES IN THE INTERPRETATION OF IMMANUEL

SIGNIFICANCE OF THE 7:14 PASSAGE

The "Immanuel section" in Isaiah has been referred to as both 7:1–9:7 and 7:1–12:6. In these chapters we see Isaiah confronting the pagan King Ahaz of Judah; the sign of God in the virgin's son, Immanuel; the predicted Assyrian invasion; the birth of Maher-shalal-hash-baz; the child who will rule on David's throne. It is interesting that children play an important role in these chapters. Three are mentioned and all three are referred to as "signs" (7:14; 8:18).

Who is Immanuel and what is his significance? His name appears in 7:14; 8:8; 8:10. To determine the proper interpretation of whom the prophet intended in these references must be considered. The 8:8 reference simply refers to Judah as Immanuel's land, and 8:10 proclaims hope because "God is with us." Did Isaiah consider this Immanuel to be already present in the land? Undoubtedly the most detail on him is given in chapter seven where the prophet states that his birth is to be a "sign." Therefore it is obvious that a proper interpretation necessitates a careful study of the 7:14 section. If there are definite clues to his identity here, they may well determine how we interpret the other references to this "wonder" child.

BACKGROUND OF THE PASSAGE

Isaiah 7:1-9

1 And it came to pass in the days of Ahaz the son of Jotham, the son of Uzziah, king of Judah, that Rezin the king of Syria, and Pekah, the son of Remaliah, king of Israel, went up to Jerusalem for war against it, but could not prevail against it.

2 And it was told the house of David, saying, Syria is resting upon Ephraim; and his heart was moved and the heart of his

25

people as the trees of the forest are moved from before the wind.

3 Then the Lord said unto Isaiah, Go out now to meet Ahaz, thou and Shear-yashub thy son, unto the end of the ascent of the upper pool, unto the way of the fuller's field.

4 And thou shall say to him, Take heed and be quiet, fear not, nor let thy heart be soft, for the two tails of these smoking firebrands, the burning anger of Rezin and Syria and of the son of Remaliah.

5 Because there has devised evil against thee Syria, Ephraim and the son of Remaliah, saying,

6 Let us go up against Judah and destroy her and let us make breaches in her for us, and let us cause a king to reign in her midst, even the son of Tabeel.

7 Thus saith the Lord God, It shall not stand neither shall it come to pass.

8 For the head of Syria is Damascus, and the head of Damascus is Rezin, and within sixty-five years will Ephraim be broken, that it be not a people.

9 And the head of Ephraim is Samaria, and the head of Samaria is Remaliah's son: if ye will not believe, it is because ye are not established.[1]

According to the information supplied by Isaiah in the above verses, Syria and the Northern Kingdom of Israel (Ephraim) had formed an alliance against Judah because of her refusal to join them in standing against powerful Assyria. Their obvious intention was to replace Ahaz with their own "puppet-king," who would cooperate with their ambitions. Fearing the invasion of his neighbors, Ahaz was inclined to call on the aid of the Assyrian conqueror, Tiglath-pileser.

According to II Kings 15:37, Syria and Ephraim had already begun siege of Judah in the days of Jotham. From II Kings 16:5, we learn that they came against Jerusalem without success, yet (according to II Chron. 28:5) Ahaz was captured and one hundred-twenty thousand of Judah were slain. There has been some difficulty over determining whether these accounts refer to the same war and, in

---

1. Translations given by Young in his *Commentary*, op. cit., p. 266.

particular, the same campaign or to different phases of the war. Most agree that both provide, at least, information about the same war. In relating the two records, it seems that the Kings passage tells the beginning and end of the siege, while Chronicles fills in the intervening events. II Kings 16 appears, therefore, to be parallel to Isaiah 7.

Rezin undoubtedly is the instigator since the verb is singular and the conjunction before Pekah indicates that "Rezin came up, together with Pekah" against Jerusalem (the principal object of their advance).[2] Having captured Ahaz, Rezin seems to have given him over to Pekah, and the spoil which had been taken from Judah was delivered to Samaria.[3]

The *New Bible Dictionary* provides this chronological chart:[4]

Kings of Judah:	Kings of Israel:	
Jotham (as ruler) 740–32	Menahem	752–42
	Pekahiah	742–40
Ahaz (as ruler) 732–15	Pekah	740–32
	Hoshea	732–23

Jotham's policy apparently had been one of independence as far as Assyria was concerned. Such, evidently, did not find favor with all of Judah. Some have speculated that it was such a pro-Assyrian group that brought Ahaz to the throne, first as co-regent in 744, then as a senior partner in 735, and finally as sole ruler in 732.[5] The year 734 B.C. has generally been accepted as the date for the prophecy given in chapter seven of Isaiah.[6]

---

2. For a discussion of the minor variations in typical Semitic writing and comparative narration see G. D. Young, *Oudtestamentische Studien*, Deel VIII, 1950, pp. 291-99.

3. See E. Young, *Commentary*, p. 267, for explanation of how the city could be saved and yet the king captured.

4. *New Bible Dictionary*, p. 220.

5. See E. Young, *Studies*, p. 146.

6. See E. Thiele, *The Mysterious Numbers of the Hebrew Kings* (Grand Rapids: Eerdmans, 1951), pp. 120ff., for a discussion of the chronology of the period. Also, Glazebrook accepts the 735–34 date, saying it cannot possibly be later, since the historical context allows us to fix the date with "unusual accuracy." In *Studies in the Book of Isaiah* (Oxford: Clarendon Press, 1910), p. 42.

At Samaria, however, the prophet Oded and certain Ephraimitic chiefs advised the return of the captives, and apparently Ahaz was also returned to Jerusalem. This did not, however, seem to deter the intentions of Rezin and Pekah, since they regrouped for further attack. What panicked Ahaz was the announcement that Syria had not returned home, but was "resting" (נָחָה) upon Ephraim, and evidently this "friendly halt" in Israelitish territory only signified evil consequences to Ahaz.[7] To him, appeal to Assyria seemed to be the only solution. If it was at this time that he decided to call on the aid of Tiglath-pileser, the Isaiah account would seem to be interspersed between the events in Kings and Chronicles, being given before Ahaz's appeal to Assyria.[8]

The purpose of Isaiah's meeting Ahaz was to dissuade him from taking a wrong course of action by relying on Assyria rather than upon Yahweh. To do so he sought to bring a word of comfort and victory to the fearful monarch. This message of hope came at a time when Ahaz thought all was hopelessly lost.

Wordsworth observes that the meeting by the upper pool is evidence that the city expected to be attacked. He writes:

> The problem before Ahaz was how to ensure the water supply of the city and to cut it off from the enemy. So long as there was access to Gihon by the Jebusite shaft the citizens might in case of siege suffer inconvenience, but not absolute lack of water.[9]

We see Isaiah coming to meet the young king[10] at the end of the conduit of the upper pool in the highway of the fuller's field, which

---

7. B. Duhm, *Das Buch Jesaia,* 1922, p. 71. He understands the form to mention "lighting upon" (as an attack). Also see E. Kraeling, "The Immanuel Prophecy," in *Journal of Biblical Literature* L (1931): 277n. Most, however, regard the expression as being of a cooperative nature. So the Revised Standard Version, 1952: "in league with."

8. See discussions by G. Smith, op. cit., pp. 110ff.; W. Wordsworth, *En Roeh: The Prophecies of Isaiah the Seer* (Edinburgh: T. & T. Clark, 1939), pp. 70ff.; W. Kelly, *An Exposition of the Book of Isaiah* (London: Hammond, n.d.), p. 121.

9. Wordsworth, op. cit., p. 73. R. Kittel also agrees in *Great Men and Movements in Israel* (New York: Macmillan, 1929), p. 266.

10. A. Gordon, *The Faith of Isaiah* (London: James Clark & Co., 1919), p. 60. He states that Ahaz is barely twenty-one years old at this time.

is west of the city.[11] Accompanying his father is Shear-Yashub ("a remnant shall return"). The significance of his presence has been overlooked by many. In chapter eight we are told that Isaiah's children are for "signs." Therefore, it would not be improper to find meaning in the boy's name, which is indicative of hope.[12] It is a striking name in which the emphasis falls upon the "remnant" rather than the "returning." The specific historical details related here emphasize God's dealing with His people in actual history. Young takes Jennings to task at this point for "spiritualizing away" these descriptions.[13]

Isaiah tells Ahaz that these two firebrands from the north are only "smoldering sticks." Though they have devised evil against the throne of David by setting up the son of Tabeel,[14] they shall not succeed, for God has other purposes for that throne.[15] The prophet then calls for faith and courage from Ahaz to receive what he is about to say.

Probably the most helpful and clear picture of the prophecy's introduction and warning is given in a chart by Raven.[16]

	SYRIA	EPHRAIM	JUDAH
AFFIR-MATION	The Head of Syria is Damascus and the Head of Damascus is Rezin.	The Head of Ephraim is Samaria and the Head of Samaria is the Son of Remaliah.	
PREDIC-TION		Within threescore and five years shall Ephraim be broken that it be not a people.	If ye believe not surely ye shall not remain.

---

11. For a contrary opinion to that of most, see E. Strachey, *Hebrew Politics in the Times of Sargon and Sennacherib* (London: Longman, Brown, Green and Longmans, 1853), p. 87. He asserts that the location is north of the city.

12. Later further examination will be considered.

13. E. Young, *Commentary*, p. 271n.

14. *Tab'el:* "Good is God." For equivalent usage see I Kings 15:18 (*tab-rimmon:* "good is Rimmon").

15. In Samuel 7:14-17 God had promised a permanent dynasty to the David throne. It was to be reserved for the coming "Anointed One."

16. J. Raven, *Emmanuel* (London: Longmans, Reader and Dyer, 1872), p. 10.

The poetic structure makes it clear that Ephraim is to fall and within sixty-five years lose all national distinction and that Judah will also fall if she does not heed God's warning.[17] Here we have the picture: Judah has begun to weaken, but Ahaz refuses to submit to his northern invaders. Rather than turn to God, he would seek the support of the Assyrian Empire. It must be remembered that Ahaz is the one who introduced the pagan altar to the temple worship. He is a man who has been deliberately disobedient to God. Only such a man, languishing in evil, could reject the promise of help from God that was about to be extended to him.

"THEREFORE"

Having denounced Ahaz for trying his and God's patience, Isaiah connects his statements recorded in verse 13 to verse 14 with the Hebrew particle לָכֵן ("therefore"). Its emphasis may be clarified by phrases such as "since this is so," "for these reasons," "according to such conditions."[18] This connective word often was used by the prophets to introduce a divine command or declaration. Young agrees with Kraeling and Hammershaimb that "the mere presence of the particle does not itself insure that the declaration to be made will be one of doom."[19]

Most commentators have not bothered to deal much with this word. Young and Budde, however, stress its relationship to verse 13. They feel it serves to introduce a "sign of a different character from that which had previously been offered."[20] Ahaz could have chosen any sign to attest God's message of hope as delivered by the prophet,

---

17. Many have emphasized the significance of this challenge by providing their own translations: G. A. Smith, "If ye have not faith, ye cannot have staith"; M. Luther, *"Glaubet ihr nicht; so bleibet ihr nicht"; J. McFayden, "No Faith, No Fixity." Quoted in A. Gordon, op. cit., p. 62n. Such attempts have led this writer to try his own hand, "If you will not confide; then you will not abide!"

18. Brown, Driver, and Briggs, *A Hebrew and English Lexicon of the Old Testament* (Oxford: University Press, 1907), p. 486.

19. E. Young, *Studies,* p. 156. In support of this Young says, "It may be the announcement of blessing" (cites Ex. 6:6; Num. 25:12; Isa. 10:24; 28:16; 29:22).

20. Ibid., p. 156.

but he refused and "therefore" God will choose His own sign to give to Ahaz.

The context in which verse 14 fits is thereby unified with the transitory word, "therefore." The worried king will not trust in God, so the impatient prophet assures him that God will give a sign to the nation of Judah that will command their trust. Since the line of David is at stake and will later even be wiped out (officially), the people will need some confidence to trust in God's maintaining the throne of David for "all generations." It is the sign of Immanuel that commands their confidence in God.

The prophet had taken a message of hope to the king, but instead he has given him a sign of both impending doom (to Judah) and ultimate hope (to the throne of David).

"SIGN"

In Scripture the word אוֹת refers to something addressed to the senses to attest the existence of divine power. Often extraordinary events were given as a sign to assure faith or to demonstrate authority. The *Interpreter's Bible* declares:

> Sign: a signal, communication. . . . It may be a natural event which becomes a sign because it is predicted, or an extraordinary or miraculous happening: a wonder.[21]

In this context many opinions have been presented as to Isaiah's usage of אוֹת.[22] Alexander has given a moderate view of the term *sign,* of which he says it is not necessarily a miracle but more a pledge of the truth of something.[23] It may be a miracle (see Isa. 38:8, Judges 6:37; Ex. 4:8) or a prediction (see Ex. 3:12; II Kings 19:29) or a symbolic name or action (see Isa. 38:18; 20:3; Ezek. 4:8). The main purpose in God's giving the sign to Ahaz was to establish

---

21. *Interpreter's Bible* (New York: Abingdon, 1958), vol. V, p. 217.

22. Fausset says "sign" implies a "miraculous token." See Jamiesson, Fausset, and Brown, op. cit., p. 437. Kraeling, "The Immanuel Prophecy," in *Journal of Biblical Literature* L (1931): 280. He believes that "something unusual" is to be looked for "so that the ancient virgin birth interpretation was not without a good psychological basis. . . ." On the other hand, Gray, op. cit., p. 124, denies that the word אוֹת or the circumstances require a miracle in the predicted event.

23. See discussion in Alexander, op cit., pp. 111-112.

the vindication of Isaiah's divine legation.

One writer has pointed out the significance of the usage of signs: "The faith that walks by signs is not by any means to be lightly esteemed. It has been allied with the highest nobility of character and achievement."[24] The *Interpreter's Dictionary of the Bible* points out that the usage of the "sign" in Isaiah 7:14 is one of assurance.[25]

It should be noted that the sign was given by the Lord (אֲדֹנָי). The covenant name (יהוה) is not used here. Usually, Isaiah uses אֲדֹנָי to emphasize the Lord's omnipotence.[26] It is only God who can give a sign whether in heaven above or Sheol below. It is such a sign that is about to be declared.

It is also important to notice that the sign is directed to "you" (plural) and is not directed to King Ahaz, as the first promise was.[27] In verse 13 Isaiah had said: "Hear ye now, O house of David," and it is apparent that the plural "you" in verse 14 is to be connected to its antecedent "ye" in verse 13, and "ye" is the "house of David." Since the context tells us that the dynasty of David is what is at stake in the impending invasion, it would seem proper to so interpret the plural "you" as the "house of David" which is the recipient of the sign.[28]

Two questions come to mind here. (1) What is the significance of the giving of the sign to the "house of David"? The context again provides the answer. Since Rezin and Pekah are seeking to eliminate the Davidic dynasty by placing the son of Tabeel on the throne, the greatest question in the minds of the royal family must have been: What will happen then to the promise of God that David's throne

---

24. Article on "Signs" in the *International Standard Bible Encyclopedia,* op. cit., p. 2789.

25. *Interpreter's Dictionary of the Bible,* p. 345, also gives other usages of "signs" as, "identifying mark, declaration, warning, reminder, lesson, omen, testimony."

26. See discussions in E. Young, *Studies,* p. 157. He speculates that the substitution of this word for Yahweh was deliberate.

27. Calvin seems to have been the first to point this out. Op. cit., p. 247.

28. E. Young, *Studies,* p. 158. He regards the address as being to all the nation. Alexander, op. cit., p. 113, says this does not imply that Isaiah turned from Ahaz to speak to the rest of the house of David, but rather that the members of the royal line were all implicated by Ahaz's unbelief.

shall be for all time? Therefore, the impending sign must be such that, since it is addressed to the house of David, it will in some way answer this question. (2) What is the significance of the sign? A. B. Simpson, the founder of the Christian and Missionary Alliance, has written a devotional commentary on Isaiah and provides these answers based on the view that the sign is a prediction of Christ. He says it is significant because of (1) the prophetic announcement and fulfillment; (2) demonstration of God's interest in human affairs; (3) indication of the supernatural character of Christianity; (4) moral significance of humility; (5) sign of God's own character and will; (6) incarnation is a pledge of the second advent.[29] Later the question of the significance of the sign to Ahaz will be discussed.

"BEHOLD"

The word הִנֵּה is used to arrest the attention. Here, Isaiah uses it to introduce Immanuel. This form of announcement is similar to Genesis 16:11, where Hagar is addressed, and to Judges 13:5, 7, which is an annunciation to the wife of Manoah. In all three cases an unusually important event is signified. The word "behold" is merely an interjection, but when used with a participle, הִנֵּה does introduce either a present or future action.[30] The question then is whether הָרָה is a participle. Young points out that the regular feminine participle would be הֹרָה and concludes that הָרָה is a verbal adjective.[31] Therefore, not much weight should be given to the usage of הִנֵּה as expressing any tense.[32]

The real importance in the use of this term seems to be its calling attention to an important birth. We are to look with anticipation to the virgin and her son. The exegete would do well to do likewise.

---

29. Simpson, *Isaiah* (Harrisburg, Pa.: Christian Publications, n.d.), pp. 89-102.

30. Delitzsch, op. cit., p. 216, regards it as always introducing a future occurrence in Isaiah. Yet in Isaiah 6:7 this does not seem to be the case.

31. E. Young, *Studies*, p. 161. He then points out that a verbal adjective should be taken as expressing present conditions.

32. Young discusses this term at length in *Studies* (1954), pp. 161-63, but reduces the significance upon it in his new work, *The Book of Isaiah* (1965), pp. 284-86.

Two important considerations then are: (1) Who is the "virgin"? (2) Who is Immanuel?

'ALMAH

Undoubtedly few words have received more extensive treatment than the form Isaiah used in this passage to represent the girl who was to bear Immanuel. Since the nineteenth century there has raged a great verbal battle over which translation of this word is the proper one: "virgin" or "maiden." Before examining the form עַלְמָה alone, a consideration of the context of verse fourteen will demonstrate the significance of the translation of that word.

The Time of Action in Verse Fourteen

It is quite important to determine whether the verbal elements of this passage indicate future or present time. The standard translation has been: ". . . shall conceive and bear a son" (KJV). Dillmann tried to hold out for the acceptance of the usage as future.[33] A study of the contextual usage of הָרָה makes this quite difficult to accept. There would be good support for interpreting this conception as a future event if the participle were used with הִנֵּה. However, the ordinary participial form would be הֹרָה. The form הָרָה is neither a verb nor a participle, but a feminine adjective connected with an active participle ("bearing") and denotes that the scene is present to the prophet's view.[34] This usage is then similar to the annunciation of the Angel of the Lord to Hagar in the wilderness: "Behold! thou art pregnant and wilt bear a son" (Gen. 16:12).[35] Thus, Isaiah's formula for announcing this birth is not uncommon to Scripture.

It is quite obvious that the verbal time indicated here should be taken as present tense, and so most since Lowth have agreed.[36]

---

33. Dillmann, op. cit., p. 70.
34. For a detailed discussion of the usages of הָרָה see Alexander, op. cit., p. 121, and Young, *Studies,* pp. 161-62. Young concludes that "the adjective should be taken as expressing present condition, unless there are compelling reasons to the contrary. Such reasons are not present in Isaiah 7:14. . . ."
35. Skinner, op. cit., p. 56, similarly translates this passage, "is with child" (present) and "shall bear" (future).
36. Lowth, op. cit., p. 70, translated this passage, "Behold, the virgin conceiveth, and beareth a son; and she shall call his name Immanuel." Cowles,

This concept of time is exceedingly important to an interpretation of the passage. If the word עַלְמָה can mean "virgin," and if this עַלְמָה is already pregnant and bearing a son, then the girl is still a virgin, even though she is a mother. The implication is that this child is miraculously born without a father, and despite pregnancy the mother is still considered to be a virgin. For, as Alexander has pointed out, if this word means virgin, then it implies only a state of present virginity, not that she will always remain a virgin.[37] If the verbal action were future tense, there would be no guarantee that the virgin who would (in the future) bear a son would still at that time be a virgin, and not a wife. But if a "virgin" "is with child" and is obviously both a virgin and a mother, we cannot escape the conclusion that this is a picture of a virgin birth.[38]

The only way out of such a conclusion is to deny that 'almah can mean a "virgin."[39] If it cannot mean virgin, the case is dismissed, but if it can mean such, there would be every reason to assert that it does in fact have this meaning. The problem now is to determine whether 'almah can or cannot mean "virgin."

The Article ה

The Hebrew definite article ה is used in connection with עַלְמָה. The usual English translation of the article is "the." Professor Lindbolm of Lund says: "The most natural explanation is that a definite woman is in view."[40] Hengstenberg felt that the relation of *hinneh* to the article in *ha'almah* is best explained by the present tense

op. cit., p. 52, also agreed that "the Hebrew words rendered 'shall conceive' and 'shall bear' are in the present tense, meaning *is* with child and *is* bringing forth. . . . The first is strictly a verbal adjective denoting a state of pregnancy and the second is the participle which is uniformly used in Hebrew for the present tense."

37. Alexander, op. cit., p. 116.

38. Kittel, op. cit., p. 270, seems to have confronted the same obstacle when he wrote, "A strange sign, the pregnancy of a woman and the name of her son! But we must remember that everything was saturated with the miraculous."

39. See the opinion of the "death-of-God" theologian, W. Hamilton, *Modern Reader's Guide to Matthew and Luke* (New York: Association Press, 1959), p. 20. He says, "The Hebrew original, 'almah cannot mean 'virgin' so we must conclude that Isaiah does not have a supernatural birth in mind."

40. S. Lindholm, *A Survey of the Immanuel Section of Isaiah* (Lund, 1958), p. 19.

of the context. So that, the girl is present to the inward perception of the prophet.[41] Birks understood it to signify the damsel of the race of David through whom the Messiah would come.[42] On the other hand, Mauchline feels that Isaiah refers only to "some woman" who will bear a child "in a few months."[43] It is unlikely that the prophet meant any woman when he specified "the" 'almah. To get around this, others have proposed that Isaiah is referring to the virgin of a popular and contemporary myth.[44] This idea has never gained wide acceptance since none seem to be able to conclusively determine which myth. Also, there is little evidence for a clear parallel to Isaiah's concept. Such an attempt, however, reveals that the force of this passage indicates that a particular person is meant by the prophet.

Young has followed Alexander in maintaining that Isaiah does not necessarily use the article to denote some well-known virgin but rather, in the generic sense, some particular, yet unknown person.[45] Whover the girl is, Isaiah must be enough aware of her distinctiveness to specify "the" 'almah; therefore, when we attempt to determine who Immanuel is, we should remember that Isaiah likely means not some vague abstraction but a definite person. 'Almah and Immanuel are both real individuals as far as Isaiah is concerned.

The Significance and Usage of עלמה

There has long been much contention over the meaning of 'almah.

---

41. Hengstenberg, *Christology*, vol. II, p. 44.
42. Birks, op. cit., p. 52.
43. Mauchline, op. cit., p. 99. However, he offers no support for his viewpoint, nor does he state how he knows she will bear a child in "a few months."
44. Gray, op. cit., p. 125, quotes Gressmann as saying that there was a popular and well-known prophecy of a young child who will deliver Judah, and that Isaiah refers to this child. However, he concludes that Gressmann's proof is weak, and it does not answer many difficulties. Mowinckel, op. cit., p. 113, says of 'almah that it is obviously "the virgin," so Isaiah must have known who she was. He feels that the only good answer is that this is a reference to a popular belief that a supernatural woman would bear a son who would bring a great transformation to Judah. For support of this he cites Usner's article on *"Milch und Honig"* in *Rheinisches Museum,* where he attempts to connect the terminology "milk and honey" to the superfood of Babylonian paradise. Such connection is weak; for further discussion see ahead in section on "Immanuel."
45. Compare E. Young, *Studies,* p. 164, and Alexander, op. cit., p. 219.

All agree that it denotes a girl or young woman above the age of childhood who has arrived at sexual maturity. The more commonly used word for virgin in the Old Testament is בְּתוּלָה . Many have contended that if Isaiah meant to say "virgin," he would have used בְּתוּלָה, and since he did not, we should reject the interpretation of עַלְמָה as "virgin."[46] Gray stated that "it asserts neither virginity nor the lack of it." He does add, though, that in actual usage it is often applied to women who are in fact virgins.[47]

Dewart long ago rightly advised that the use of a word, not its etymology, determines its meaning.[48] It is true that 'almah is not the common word for virgin, but its employment always denotes a virgin. The word עַלְמָה occurs in Scripture five times in the plural and four times in the singular.[49]

Biblical Usage. The plural form, עֲלָמוֹת, appears in Song of Solomon 1:3. "For the savour of thy good ointments, oil poured out is thy name, therefore 'Alāmōth have loved thee." The virgins in the harem are here distinguished from the queens (wives). It is the bride who is speaking here praising her husband. For this reason the virgins in the harem have loved him and desired a husband. It is clear that the 'alāmōth in this passage are not married women. In Song of Solomon 6:8 we read: "Sixty are the queens, eighty the concubines, and 'alāmōth without number." The author here defines

---

46. For example see the *Interpreter's Bible*, p. 218. It is interesting to note that the exegetical section supports a denial of the miraculous virgin birth, while the expositional section affirms it on the same page! Perhaps Kilpatrick forgot to heed Scott's warning that an inaccurate translation of the LXX by the New Testament must not "prejudice" our interpretation. It might be well for the editors to get together on their hermeneutics!

47. Gray, op. cit., pp. 126-27.

48. Dewart, op. cit., p. 123. Therefore, Cheyne, op. cit., pp. 140-41, in discussing the relationship of עַלְמָה to עָלַם ("to hide"), warns that we not force a connection that is not an actual derivation. He is not convinced that the Arabic parallel *ḥabat* ("girl") is related to *ḥabaa* ("to hide in a tent") as 'almah is "to hide" (conceal, as a virgin) in Hebrew. He says that he favors the translation "young woman" but that the usage of 'almah in the Old Testament seems to favor an unmarried woman. On the other hand, Boutflower, op. cit., p. 47n., says that 'almah comes from the root meaning "to be mature" and points more to being of marriageable age than virginity. He too, however, adds that the Old Testament attestations seem to always mean "virgin."

49. For the most definitive and well-organized study of these passages, see E. Young, *Studies*, pp. 171-77.

his usage of the term by distinguishing the different classes. It is quite clear that these "maidens" are unmarried girls. In Psalm 68:25 the use of *'alāmōth* is not as clear to determine whether or not they are married: "The singers went before, afterwards the players on stringed instruments; in the midst of *'alāmōth* striking timbrels." The reference in this passage does not indicate that they are virgins, nor does it imply that they are not. Likewise the instruction to the singers (*'alāmōth*) in I Chronicles 15:20 and Psalm 46:1 does not limit the meaning in any way.

In the reference to Rebekah in Genesis 24:43, Abraham's servant has been sent to find a wife for Isaac. Naturally, he is seeking an unmarried virgin. We are also told in this chapter that Rebekah is a "virgin" (*bethūlah*) and she had not had sexual relations with any man. It is apparent that the word עַלְמָה may suitably be applied to a girl who is a virgin. In Exodus 2:8 Miriam is also described as an עַלְמָה . It is almost certain that she was only a little girl at this time, patiently waiting as her mother had commanded her.[50] Therefore *'almah* is again used here of an unmarried girl. In Proverbs 30:19 the writer expresses four things that are "too wonderful" for him: the way of an eagle in the air, the way of a serpent upon the rock, the way of a ship in the midst of the sea, and the way of a man with a *'almah*. In verse twenty he then contrasts the evil woman to the virtuous maiden. Unfortunately, Young interprets this reference as to an evil girl, who is, nevertheless, not married.[51]

However, two things must be noticed here. First, the condition of the *'almah* is essential to the interpretation of Isaiah 7:14. Whether or not she is married (legally) is not the question here, for a maiden practicing fornication could just as easily become a mother and, if that were the case in Proverbs, why could it not be the same in Isaiah? Secondly, the passage here indicates nothing evil about the "way of a man with a maid." He parallels it to the natural events of a bird in flight, the speed of a snake, and a ship floating on water.

---

50. O. Allis, *Revised Version or Revised Bible?* (Philadelphia: Presbyterian and Reformed, 1953), p. 45. He mentions that this account indicates that the girl was still living with her parents and was under their jurisdiction, and therefore was most probably not married.

51. E. Young, *Studies*, pp. 176-77.

These things amaze him, as does the way of a man with a maid. The meaning here is obviously that of the natural attraction and affection of men for girls. The expression is not one of lust, but of the mystery of wonderful human affection. The juxtaposition of the next verses by the compiler provides a contrast between the natural blessing of the virtuous maid and the evil of the adulterous woman. Therefore, the picture here should be taken as that of a virgin maid.

Though the usage of עַלְמָה in the Old Testament is not always definitely defined as a virgin, it is never used of a married woman and is sometimes defined as a virgin.

Non-Biblical Usage. Much has been said of the Ras Shamra tablets that refer to the marriage between Nikkal and Yarih.[52] Here the technical term for "virgin" is *btl* (cf. *bethūlah*), while the parallel expression is *ǵlmt*. Both terms are applied to the yet unmarried Nikkal. Therefore, it appears that the two terms are used synonomously in Ras Shamra literature. Though *ǵlmt* (cf. *'almah*) is not the common word for "virgin" in Ugaritic, it is never used in Ras Shamra of a married woman and seems well suited for application to a woman who is not yet married.

Also in the "Legend of Keret" the marriage of Keret to Hry shows that the term *ǵlmt*, though applied to Hry before the wedding, is never used of her afterwards. Young has concluded that there is no evidence in any of the Ras Shamra material that lends support to the claim that *'almah* may be used of a married woman.[53]

Having surveyed Hebrew legal contracts and documents, Robert Dick Wilson came to a similar conclusion. He summarized:

> Finally, two conclusions from the evidence seem clear; first, that *'almah,* so far as is known, never meant "young married woman"; and, secondly, since the presumption in common law was and is, that every *'almah* is a virgin and virtuous, until she be proven not to be, we have a right to assume that Rebekah and the *'almah* of Isaiah 7:14 and all other *'almahs* were virgins.[54]

---

52. For a thorough discussion of this evidence see E. Young, *Studies,* pp. 166-70. For a detailed survey of extra-biblical occurrences of *'almah* and its equivalents see C. Gordon, *Ugaritic Handbook,* III, p. 220, and W. LaSor, *Isaiah 7:14—"Young Woman" or "Virgin"?*, p. 4.

53. E. Young, *Studies,* p. 169.

54. Wilson, "The Meaning of 'Almah (A.V. 'Virgin') in Isaiah VII.14," in *The Princeton Theological Review* XXIV (1926): 316.

Finally, consider the evaluation of non-biblical evidence by the eminent Jewish scholar Cyrus Gordon:

> The commonly held view that "virgin" is Christian, whereas "young woman" is Jewish is not quite true. The fact is that the Septuagint, which is the Jewish translation made in pre-Christian Alexandria, takes 'almah to mean "virgin" here. Accordingly, the New Testament follows Jewish interpretation in Isaiah 7:14. Little purpose would be served in repeating the learned expositions that Hebraists have already contributed in their attempt to clarify the point at issue. It all boils down to this: the distinctive Hebrew word for "virgin" is betulah, whereas 'almah means a "young woman" who may be virgin, but is not necessarily so. The aim of this note is rather to call attention to a source that has not yet been brought into the discussion. From Ugarit of around 1400 B.C. comes a text celebrating the marriage of the male and female lunar deities. It is there predicted that the goddess will bear a son. . . . The terminology is remarkably close to that in Isaiah 7:14. However, the Ugaritic statement that the bride will bear a son is fortunately given in parallelistic form; in 77:7 she is called by the exact etymological counterpart of Hebrew 'almah "young woman"; in 77:5 she is called by the exact etymological counterpart of Hebrew betulah "virgin." Therefore, the New Testament rendering of 'almah as "virgin" for Isaiah 7:14 rests on the older Jewish interpretation, which in turn is now borne out for precisely this annunciation formula by a text that is not only pre-Isaianic but is pre-Mosaic in the form that we now have it on a clay tablet.[55]

Conclusion. It is quite obvious from a consideration of the usage of עַלְמָה that there is little basis for denying that it means one who is in fact a virgin.[56] Two writers have well summarized their conclusions. Machen says:

> It may be readily admitted that *almah* does not actually indicate virginity, as does *bethūlah;* it means rather "a young woman of marriageable age." But on the other hand one may well doubt,

---

55. C. Gordon, *"Almah* in Isaiah 7:14," *Journal of Bible and Religion* XXI (April, 1953): 106.

56. Young, *Studies*, p. 183. He challenges those who claim it can refer to a married woman to offer proof to substantiate such a claim. Cf. Archer, "Isaiah," in *W.B.C.*, p. 618. He agrees that the contextual usage demonstrates that the *'almah* "refers only to a maiden chaste and unmarried."

in view of the usage, whether it was a natural word to use of anyone who was not in point of fact a virgin.[57]

Hanke adds a very pertinent observation:

> The only basis for saying that *almah* is not the regular term for virgin is that it is not the common term. . . . The evidence indicates also that had Isaiah wished to say "young woman" he would have chosen the term *Na'arah,* the term which the RSV usually translates as "young woman."[58]

Consider also that the ordinary word for "virgin," בְּתוּלָה does not itself guarantee by its usage that its referent is in fact a virgin. In Deuteronomy 22:19 and Joel 1:8 *bethūlah* refers to a married woman. Dr. Knight of McCormick Theological Seminary admits that the usage of *bethūlah* in Joel 1:8 ("Lament like a 'virgin,' girded in sackcloth for the husband of her youth") cannot mean that she is unmarried, for she is already a widow; therefore, the term *bethūlah* does not itself give absolute expression that the maiden is always in fact a virgin.[59] Therefore, if Isaiah wished to use a word that would exactly express his intention, the use of *'almah* would better signify virginity than would the more common term *bethūlah.*[60]

Vine has also pointed to another distinction between these two appellations. *Bethūlah* usually signifies a maiden living with her parents and whose marriage was not impending, while *'almah* denotes one who is mature and ready for marriage.[61]

It is quite obvious that if Isaiah intended to convey a prediction of the virgin birth he chose the right word, not an improper one.

---

57. J. G. Machen, *The Virgin Birth of Christ* (New York: Harper & Brothers, 1930), p. 288.

58. H. Hanke, *The Validity of the Virgin Birth* (Grand Rapids: Zondervan, 1963), p. 24.

59. G. Knight, *A Christian Theology of the Old Testament* (London: SCM Press, 1964), p. 309.

60. One cannot help but wonder what the deniers of the virgin birth prediction would say if Isaiah had used the term *bethūlah.* Would they readily agree that this was such a prediction or would they point to Joel 1:8 and say, not so, it can also mean a married woman, therefore, do not force Isaiah to say what he is not saying!!

61. For support of this view see W. Vine, *Isaiah: Prophecies, Promises, Warning* (London: Oliphants, 1953), p. 35; and Archer, op. cit., p. 618. He states, "In actual usage in the Hebrew Scriptures, however, it refers only to a maiden chaste and unmarried (so far as the context shows)."

There is no basis for asserting that he should have used another word in place of *'almah*. Usage indicates that *'almah* is the most correct term to use to signify an unmarried virgin.

Our conclusion must contradict those who say *'almah* "cannot" mean virgin. It most obviously can and most probably always does. Now fit the evidence together: If *'almah* means "virgin," and if the time of pregnancy in verse 14 is present, so that the girl is presently both pregnant and a virgin, it must be concluded that she is none other than the only virgin mother in biblical history: Mary, the mother of Jesus! Most of the evidence thus far indicates that the highest probability is that Isaiah is predicting the birth of Christ in the 7:14 passage.

The Identity of the Virgin

Certainly many have not accepted the above statement, for Isaiah's *'almah* has been variously identified as anyone from his own wife to an anonymous maid standing by and looking on.[62] Consider briefly some of the more popular attempts at identification.

(1) Prophet's own wife. She is called the "prophetess" in 8:3. Isaiah has one son with him, Shear-yashub. The coming Immanuel would then have to be Maher-shalal-hash-baz.[63] This view is best represented by Dr. Gleason Archer. Most earlier writers attempted to support this view by relating the prophet's wife to the "fact" that the *'almah* was not a "virgin." Dr. Archer accepts the evidence supporting the interpretation of *'almah* as "virgin" and raises the view that the prophet's wife was not married to him at the time of the 7:14 passage. Therefore, he sees the virgin in chapter seven as the

---

62. Mauchline, op. cit., pp. 98-99, not wishing to commit himself, says only that she is "some woman" who will bear a child. Knight, op. cit., pp. 309-10, says she is Hezekiah's young wife about to bear an heir to the throne. W. Thompson, *The Great Argument* (New York: Harper & Brothers, 1884), p. 199, says that she is some contemporary virgin who is about to be married and bear a son. Leslie, op. cit., p. 49, maintains that she is one of Ahaz's wives. These viewpoints are only representative of many that have been promoted.

63. An exception would be Jennings' view that the prophet has three "prophetic" sons, as did Hosea, and that Immanuel is to be Isaiah's third son. See F. Jennings, *Studies in Isaiah* (New York: Loizeau Brothers, 1950), p. 85.

prophet's fiancee, who becomes the type of the virgin Mary, who is the ultimate fulfillment of the prophecy.[64]

(2) The queen, wife of Ahaz. One can easily see how this view could gain acceptance. For Ahaz's son Hezekiah was to become one of Judah's greatest leaders. However, even under his reign the nation began to crumble. Hezekiah is unlikely because he was already born at this time. Even further, if Ahaz's wife is meant, why should he allow her to name the child when it was common practice for the husband to do so.[65]

(3) Hezekiah's wife. Knight gets credit for this one, and one has to admit it is different.[66] He asserts that the 'almah is Hezekiah's young wife. Others have argued that Hezekiah is Immanuel! It is quite difficult to understand how a "messianic son" born to Hezekiah could be represented here. There is no evidence that Hezekiah is yet married, and Isaiah indicates that Hezekiah's heir comes late in life.[67] Also, Hezekiah's son Manesseh was characteristic of anything but "God with us."[68]

(4) An unknown on-looker. Since it is difficult to identify the 'almah because her name is not given, some have conjectured that Isaiah merely pointed to a nearby pregnant girl who was a spectator, and that as her son was born it was a sign to Ahaz.[69] Dewart and

---

64. There is an admitted parallel of functional similarity between Immanuel, God's "sign," and Isaiah's sons who were given as "signs" (8:18). Cf. Archer, op. cit., p. 618.

65. See discussion in D. Mace, *Hebrew Marriage* (1953), pp. 172-74. Exceptions seem to include Jacob's children, who were named by his wives.

66. Knight, op. cit., pp. 309-10.

67. Thus, the reason for Hezekiah's great consternation over his imminent death: he has not yet an heir to bring to the throne of David. Thus, he pleads for an extension of life and is granted fifteen extra years (see Isa. 38).

68. He seems uncertain of the identification because he also refers to the coming Word in flesh (as ultimate fulfillment?). He reveals his neo-orthodox bent when he disregards the historical significance and alludes to the name which is "the theologically important word in this context" (seems to accept Kittel's concept that some words of Scripture are "theological" and some are not). Thus he looks for the "theological significance" in a name given to Hezekiah's son and not in the son himself.

69. Mowinckel, op. cit., p. 111, is so strong on this point that he says a direct Christological interpretation is "out of the question." Why? He adds, "because the sign is intended to make Ahaz believe absolutely in *Yahweh*, surrender himself to Him in complete trust and obedience, and in virtue of

Cheyne have replied that this is highly unlikely.[70] There is no evidence of any such girl and her child in the Old Testament. Besides, it is highly unlikely that the birth of an ordinary child to an unknown woman would constitute a "sign" to Ahaz. Of all the views that deny that the virgin Mary is meant here, however, this one has the least historical problems.

Finally, the common interpretation of this passage has long been that the 'almah is the mother of Jesus who, incarnated, is "God with us." If the 'almah is a virgin who is pregnant and yet still a virgin, not having a husband, it is difficult to arrive at any other conclusion than that this is a reference to a virgin birth, which, being humanly impossible, could only be an act of God.[71] In further sections we will consider the developing interpretation of the 'almah.[72] There are very good indications for the acceptance of the view that the virgin is none other than the foreseen Mary of the New Testament. Cooper has well summarized:

> A study of the entire context of this statement shows that the prophet foresaw the coming of one of the Divine Personalities to earth in the form of a little child, born of a virgin.[73]

The Theological Implications of the Virgin Birth and the Incarnation

The dual concepts of incarnation and the virgin birth are actually interdependent upon each other. One cannot exist without the other, so that a virgin birth implies an act of God, and the incarnation like-

---

this choice to decide to adopt the right attitude in the contemporary situation, it is clear that the sign must come to pass soon. . . ." If this were the case, what happened? Why did not the sign produce this result? Where is any evidence of Ahaz's "faith," "surrender," "complete trust," "obedience," or "right attitude"? The evidence negates the argument. For a more complete discussion see ahead in the section, "Significance of the Sign of Ahaz."

70. Dewart, op. cit., p. 121, and Cheyne, op. cit., pp. 140-41.

71. Even W. Hamilton, op. cit., pp. 20-21, writing in 1959, does not deny the virgin birth itself, but only that Isaiah predicted it.

72. Skinner, op. cit., p. 63, provides a good brief survey of pre-Christian interpretation beginning with the Jewish development of an eschatological hope in the Messiah that was not exhausted by contemporary circumstances.

73. D. Cooper, *Messiah: His Redemptive Career* (Los Angeles: Biblical Research Society, 1935), p. 70. See also his interesting observation on p. 79 that in the reference in Isaiah 49:1-13, the Servant speaks of his mother but says nothing of a father. A most significant omission.

wise most naturally necessitates a virgin birth to bring the Eternal into the temporal confines of man. Thus, the virgin birth is the "act of the living God bringing the Messianic order into history."[74] Hence, it is only by God's direct action that the kingdom aspirations will ever be a realization. Therefore, the real significance of the "sign" of the virgin's son is that no help would come to Ahaz from the perverted house of David, whose wicked generations would soon perish. Only through an unmarried virgin could such help come to the Davidic line.[75] Therefore it becomes the miracle by which God also inserted Jesus into the lineage of David and furnishes a prototype for the grafting of the branches of the wild olive into the ancient tree of Israel (Rom. 11:17). Thus Christian believers become the "children of Abraham" by God's free grace, though they are not of physical Jewish descent.[76]

Otto Piper has well expressed the theological significance of the virgin birth to the Christian:

> Unless one has comprehended the virgin birth as the miraculous basis of his salvation he will either underrate the completeness and radicality with which the transformation of his predicament has taken place in faith or he will ascribe to human potentiality what is possible only as the work of God in us.[77]

---

74. W. Robinson, "A Re-Study of the Virgin Birth of Christ," *Evangelical Quarterly* XXXVII, 4 (October, 1965): 203.

75. See discussion in Lenski, op. cit., p. 53.

76. See the excellent discussion by W. Robinson, loc. cit., p. 203. Also note his study of the New Testament teaching on the virgin birth, especially the sources of Paul's references to Jesus as the "Son of God," pp. 198-211.

77. O. Piper, "Virgin Birth: the Meaning of the Gospel Accounts," *Interpretation* XVII (April, 1964): 148. Since this paper is not intended to be a study of the miraculous aspect of the incarnation and the virgin birth (only the prediction of such), see S. Johnson, "Genesis of Jesus," *Bibliotheca Sacra* 122 (October, 1965): 331-42, for a good discussion of the miraculous element of the virgin birth. For a good study of the problems involved in the study of the incarnation, see J. Walvoord, "Incarnation of the Son of God," *Bibliotheca Sacra* 117 (January, 1960): 3-12. For a good discussion on the church fathers' interpretation as reflected in the great creeds and the conflicts involved at Nicea and Chalcedon in relation to Athanasius and the Ebionites, see B. Skard, *The Incarnation* (Minneapolis: Augsburg, 1960). For a different view than the usual see W. Walker, *The Spirit and the Incarnation* (Edinburgh: T. & T. Clark, 1899), pp. 300-02. He hesitates to take a definite stand on the virgin birth at first, saying that it is hard to deny but also hard to be-

IMMANUEL

The main thrust of Isaiah's statement is undoubtedly the name of the child: עִמָּנוּ אֵל ("God with us"). Most commentators of every sort agree that the real significance is in the name and its symbolic meaning.[78] The Jewish scholar, Cyrus Gordon, maintains that the precedent of naming "symbolic children" was established by Hosea and was followed by later prophets, notably Isaiah.[79] According to the well-established usage in Isaiah, such names indicate what the person in reality is or what he represents, rather than merely his proper name.[80] Pedersen says:

> For the Israelites there is upon the whole no difference whatsoever, between the idea, the name or the matter itself, and this has also been implied by what has been said of the idea. It is not an abstraction, but the very reality underlying the momentary manifestations; it is wholly in all that belongs to it, both in the detail, in the name and the idea.[81]

Baron picks up this same concept and maintains that all of Messiah's titles were intended only as description of His character, but His real name was, in the providence of God, concealed till His advent to prevent imposture on the part of pretenders.[82] Therefore, the name, in its proper designation, was not arbitrary but characteristic of the individual.[83]

The name "God is with us" may imply two things. If taken messianically, that He is personally among us. If taken as a promise of blessing, that He is with us in the sense that He blesses us through some great individual.

---

lieve. He proceeds to attempt to show that the incarnation was an "evolutionary process" since "an irruption of the spiritual and Divine into the physical and natural sphere is so out of harmony with the idea of evolution . . . as to be incredible" (p. 402).

78. See Cheyne, op. cit., p. 47, and C. Gordon, *Introduction to Old Testament Times* (Ventor, N. J.: Ventor Press, 1953), p. 210.

79. Ibid.

80. See Cowles, op. cit., p. 52.

81. J. Pedersen, *Israel: Its Life and Culture* (London: Oxford University Press, 1926), vol. I.

82. Baron, op. cit., p. 38n.

83. See the excellent discussion by Orelli, op. cit., p. 53, on the Hebrew use of proper names.

Identification of Immanuel

Many identifications have been proposed for the Immanuel. Klausner, the former professor of Hebrew literature at the Hebrew University in Israel, maintains that Isaiah spoke here of Hezekiah, who would usher in a golden age. However, he admits that when this did not become a complete reality the prophet looked to the future for a more complete fulfillment of this hope.[84] The theory that the child Immanuel was Hezekiah is fairly widely accepted, although others have attempted to identify him with distant echoes of the Egyptian mythology about Horus and Osiris.[85] There is, however, little support for this concept since no definite parallels can be made, nor does the context of Isaiah (so closely related to actual historical events) fit such a hypothesis.[86]

Others have maintained that the child is the prophet's own son, and that the mother is the prophet's wife.[87] However, we have no recorded evidence of such a birth to his family, unless we take this

---

84. J. Klausner, *The Messianic Idea in Israel* (New York: Macmillan, 1955), pp. 56-57. Many disagree, maintaining that the birth of Immanuel can hardly be that of Hezekiah. Cheyne, op. cit., p. 48, feels that he would have already been at least nine years old by then (cf. II Kings 16:2; 18:2). Lowth, op. cit., p. 230, also agreed that Hezekiah must have already been born. G. Jelf, *Messiah Cometh* (London: Innes & Co., 1899), p. 120, maintains that Hezekiah was 10 years old. However, this remains to be adequately proven. Both F. F. Bruce, *Israel and the Nations* (Grand Rapids: Eerdmans, 1963), p. 229, and S. J. Schultz, *The Old Testament Speaks* (New York: Harper & Row, 1960), p. 154, place Ahaz on the throne in 735 B.C. Schultz has Hezekiah on the throne in 722 B.C. and Bruce in 721 B.C. Ahaz was only twenty when he came to the throne, and Israel and Syria attacked immediately. Since he reigns only sixteen years and Hezekiah is twenty-five by *c.* 721 B.C. (Ahaz is only 36!), H. Lindsell, ed., *Harper Study Bible* (RSV) (New York: Harper & Row, 1963), p. 558, dates Hezekiah's actual ascendancy at 715 B.C., after a co-regency, making Ahaz 42-43. Therefore, Hezekiah perhaps was born when Ahaz was 18 (two years before the Isaiah prophecy). However, if we subtract 715 from 735, Hezekiah would be 5 years old!

85. R. Kittel, *Die hellenistische Mysterienreligion und das Alte Testament* (Stuttgart, 1924), pp. 1-80, argues in favor of this concept by connecting the child eating "curds and honey" with the Egyptian mythology that eventually found its way into the Canaanite and Greek "mystery religions."

86. For a good criticism of Kittel's view, see Klausner, op. cit., p. 65. He rejects any concept of "dependence" as being "read *into*" the text. He declares, "In my opinion these proposals [of Kittel] have no weight."

87. Discussed by Mauchline, op. cit., pp. 98-99.

reference to be of Maher-shalal-hash-baz. His name, though implying God's assistance in victory, is not the same expression as "God
with us," and actually expresses judgment ("the prey hastens—the
spoil speeds"). Besides, if his wife were already married to him,
she can hardly be designated 'almah. A good case has been established for this viewpoint on the basis that she was not married to him
at the time of the giving of the 7:14 prophecy.[88] This view answers
some of the difficult problems involved in interpreting the passage.
The "virgin" is not taken as being presently pregnant and the prophet's son fits better with the significance of the "butter and honey"
statement.*

Two questions arise here. How can the prediction of the birth of
the prophet's own son be of great significance to Ahaz? In chapter
seven the magnitude of the sign offered to Ahaz seems to imply more
than the mere birth of the prophet's child. Also, are we certain the
"prophetess" is a recent bride in chapter eight? There are approxi-
mately twenty-five references in the Old Testament that speak of a
woman being in conception and bearing a child. Generally the formula, "he went in unto her and she conceived," is used. The girl is always identified in the immediate context as the man's wife by the
term wife, so that the reader knows who she is and why he is per-
mitted to go in to her. The only exceptions to the use of "wife" in
this formula are when the man and woman have been married for a
long time and the reader knows she is his wife (cf. Abraham and
Sarah [Gen. 21:2]; Jacob and Leah [Gen. 29:32] Jacob and Rachel
[Gen. 30:23]; the Shunammite woman [II Kings 4:17]) or when the
girl involved is not really the man's legal wife (cf. Abraham and
Hagar [Gen. 16:4]; Judah and Shuah [Gen. 38:3]; Judah and Tamar
[Gen. 38:18]; David and Bathsheba [II Sam. 11:5]). Since we are
not told that the prophetess is Isaiah's wife, are we not to assume
that they have been married a long time? Certainly this would be a
legitimate marriage. The implication, then, is that she is probably
the same mother of the older son, Shear-yashub, and therefore cannot be the 'almah of chapter seven.

Stenning tried to read Immanuel out of the text altogether. He

---

88. Archer, op. cit., pp. 618-19.
*See note 101.

proposed the variant reading of יִשְׂרָאֵל for עִמָּנוּ אֵל.[89] However, no major translations have ever followed this rendering, and the Dead Sea Scroll of Isaiah, which is the oldest copy we possess, supports the reading, "Immanuel." Others have merely avoided any identification by saying he is the son of an anonymous girl who is standing nearby.[90] Yet, they fail to say who he is or how his birth affected the present situation.

Perhaps a more sensible position for those who reject any Christological interpretation of Immanuel is the one taken by Gray, who saw in the naming of the child merely a recognition of coming blessing and deliverance.[91] So that the naming will be commensurate with all children born to mothers, who will name them after the deliverance from Syria and Israel. However, such a view seems to neglect the reference to a singular הָעַלְמָה and really does not give a sign of a promise of victory, but only that after the victory will children be named for the already attained victory.

Messianic Identification of the Child

G. A. Smith reminds us that to an Oriental mind the "Ideal Kingdom" was always connected to an "Ideal King."[92] He maintains that the name of the child is evidently the key part of the sign, and both must be explained in relation to each other. "It is hardly possible," he continues, "to dissociate the birth of the boy called Immanuel . . . from the public expectation of a King of glory."[93] Because of the close association of Immanuel with the land in chapter eight, he sees a definite connection between him and the Prince of Four Names in chapter nine, concluding that Immanuel may well be the promised Messiah of Israel. The description of Immanuel

---

89. Stenning, *The Targum of Isaiah* (London: Oxford University Press, 1949), p. 25.

90. Mauchline, loc. cit., p. 99, refutes this concept as being unlikely since the birth of an unimportant child could hardly be a great sign. He, however, declines to make any identification, saying only that he is "some child" of "some woman" but cannot tell who.

91. Gray, op. cit., p. 124.

92. G. A. Smith, *The Book of Isaiah* (New York: Harper & Brothers, 1927), vol. I, p. 131.

93. Ibid., p. 131.

bringing peace to the land and the ascriptions to the Prince of Peace in this section do seem to indicate a quality far above human imperfection. Orelli comments:

> Divine wisdom, divine energy, divine constancy of fatherly love, divine righteousness with divine peace are expressly ascribed to him so that He Himself, His own person as divine, seems raised far above humanity, and his dominion consequently is really God's dominion upon earth.[94]

The purpose of Immanuel seems to be the guarantee for the perpetuity of the endangered throne of David.[95] Ahaz is given the promise that Syria and Ephraim will not overcome his land. In some way his birth is to indicate this deliverance.[96] It is difficult to disconnect the description of the child's growth from the deliverance of Judah. Ahaz is told by Isaiah that before the child could grow to discern right from wrong the land would be forsaken of these kings from the north.[97] Gordon maintains that this indicates at least two years by the child's growing to the age of discernment.[98] The problem in the messianic interpretation is how this can relate to Christ, since He was born much later. Young replies that His birth and growth, though in prediction, are a picture of the brief time until destruction will come upon Judah's enemies.[99] How is this possible? Cowles reminds us that Isaiah saw a vision of the future event as it happened and spoke as though the child were growing before his very eyes, so that he carries over the "present condition" of the vision to the con-

---

94. Orelli, op. cit., p. 69.

95. So concludes J. Orr, *The Problem of the Old Testament* (New York: Scribner's Sons, 1907), p. 461.

96. Jelf, op. cit., p. 120, says, "The prophecy evidently points to a supernatural birth within David's family, for otherwise the perpetuity of that family would not be guaranteed; and to a birth ensuring God's Own presence with the people; and to the birth of One who not only represents God, but is God as the ninth chapter describes him."

97. So Lowth, op. cit., p. 230, maintained that within the time a virgin could conceive and bear a son and he were able to grow to the age of discernment, the enemies of Judah would be destroyed.

98. Gordon, loc. cit., p. 222.

99. E. Young, *Studies,* pp. 196-98. He states, "The language of the prophecy is filled with mystery and even with obscurity . . . but is language of profound and beautiful symbolism."

temporary situation.[100] The infancy of this child will symbolize the fact that the desolation of Judah at Ahaz's time will be short-lived, for the enemy kings will soon be rendered powerless.[101] Yet, to Ahaz will come an even greater danger, the king of Assyria. Therefore, the

---

100. Cowles, op. cit., p. 55. Also see Yates, *Essentials of Biblical Hebrew* (New York: Harper & Row, 1954), pp. 134-35, for a discussion of the "Perfect of Prophecy" used by the prophet to portray confidence in the certainty of the fulfillment of his prediction.

101. This interpretation recognizes the reference to "butter and honey" as indicating impoverishment. This has received much comment. Many see it as a reference to prosperity (see Gray, op. cit., p. 124); others try to relate it to Egyptian or Babylonian mythology (see Mauchline, op. cit., p. 99). Vine, op. cit., pp. 35-36, however, points to the context noting that instead of a prosperous farm there is only "a young cow and two sheep," and instead of a flourishing vineyard, only "briers and thorns." Alexander, op. cit., p. 114, also agrees that the picture here is one of desolation. Many have related this reference to the child who will eat "butter and honey" in 7:22. The implication is that a literal child will actually go through the period of devastation immediately ahead in which this food of privation will be common to all. Cf. Fitch, op. cit., p. 570, and Archer, *W.B.C.*, p. 618. Birks, op. cit., p. 54, holds that the land was to pass through a change from tillage to pasturage, and not until then should the Deliverer appear, whom the prophet sees as growing up from infancy amidst the shadows of ruin. Cowles, op. cit., p. 59, says the person eating "butter and honey" in vs. 22 is the man mentioned in vs. 21, who is representative of all the land. In vs. 15 he says that the prophet is merely carrying the image of the present tense as though he sees the Messiah actually growing. Delitzsch, op. cit., p. 221, takes the reference to be a time indicator parallel to the child's reaching the age of discretion. E. Young, op. cit., takes the "butter and honey" reference to mean "royal food" that Immanuel will eat because the land has been spared and the throne is not lost. This view does not seem to properly consider the reference in 7:22. Rather, the picture here is one of a "corporate concept" in this aspect of the prediction. Isaiah speaks of the Messiah's future birth with such certainty that he uses the present tense. He goes on to declare that the whole land of Judah will be destroyed by Ahaz's lack of faith. The devastation would leave the land in poverty in less time than it could take for the child to grow to the age of discernment. This provided a time-indication of how soon destruction would come. Yet, the Messiah was to issue from Judah when sifted and judged by world powers, and he would literally grow up in lowliness and poverty. The Assyrian invasions were the beginning of judgment, and were a sign that the Deliverer was near. The days of coming judgment were such that Judah never recovered her former prosperity. Thus, when the Messiah was born he grew up in a poverty-stricken land that had suffered many successive judgments. These sufferings are "corporately" here in view while the reference to Immanuel is future, just as his birth is future (in vs. 14), though it is prophetically spoken of as present.

prophecy does have significance and relevance to Ahaz; he is to avoid the attempted alliance with Assyria, for it will later cause more problems than it solves.

Vine sees the relationship of this matter to the actual birth of Christ at a later time when he writes:

> An outstanding feature of Old Testament prophecies is that they connect events chronologically separated. Conditions more immediately relating to Assyria were developed under subsequent powers successively, culminating in the Roman, under which Immanuel was born. The circumstances depicted by Isaiah as prevailing in the land continued up to and in Immanuel's day.[102]

It must be admitted that this point is the weakest link in the single-fulfillment view. The concept of the original Immanuel being the prophet's son fits somewhat better the situation herein. Yet, other difficulties with the double-fulfillment views seem to indicate that the fulfillment is singular. Either the prophet sees Christ in the future and speaks of His infancy as though He were presently growing, or he speaks of Christ and also another child whom he sees growing in the near future.

Isaiah sees with eyes of faith the potential birth of Immanuel as a present reality. The problem has been raised that if "Immanuel" is Jesus, why did He not use this name in His public ministry?[103] Yet, many names were attributed to Jesus Christ which were descriptions of Him, rather than titles that He used and were used of Him, but not by Him. Solomon too was the name Jedidiah ("beloved of the Lord") in II Samuel 12:24-25, yet he never went by that name publicly; in fact, we see no further mention of it.[104]

The reference in chapter seven, therefore, seems to indicate a messianic significance. If not, Isaiah's premature expectations for Hezekiah or for the birth of his own son must have been a great "let-down" to him. For, despite improvement, Judah still remained hampered by the Assyrian invaders because the alliance Hezekiah's

---

102. Vine, op. cit., p. 35.
103. This problem is discussed at length by Baron, op. cit., p. 38.
104. See the fine article on "Solomon" by C. E. DeVries in *Zondervan Pictorial Bible Dictionary* (Grand Rapids: Zondervan, 1963), p. 801.

father made with them also brought subjection and vassalage.[105] The monarchy soon crumbled under Hezekiah's son, and man's most valiant efforts could not save the throne and kingdom of David. Only the action of God could bring to the forefront His true King: the Messiah of Israel, Jesus Christ.

CONTEMPORARY SIGNIFICANCE OF THE "SIGN" TO AHAZ

When maintaining that Isaiah's Immanuel is a direct reference to Christ and only to Him, one may well be asked what possible significance could such a sign have to Ahaz (or the house of David) and how are we to interpret the development of the child in relation to this consideration? This problem has led many to see the need for a contemporary fulfillment of this prophecy in Ahaz's time.[106]

It is interesting to note that this introduction of Immanuel is at a time when the throne of Israel is threatened more than it has ever been. In a previous section several references were given showing that the person Immanuel is the purpose of the prophetic utterance. Significance may be seen in the term *virgin*, but it is actually Immanuel to whom the prophet calls attention. As many have said, it is not only the name that is significant of this child, but that name is a revelation of His character and being.

It must be remembered that Isaiah does not direct the sign to Ahaz but to the "house of David" (you-plural). Because of this many feel that there need be no "significance" to Ahaz himself.[107] How-

---

105. Thus, Tiglath-Pileser's victory inscription lists Ahaz as a vassal paying tribute and homage to him. Therefore, Kirkpatrick, op. cit., p. 162, saw not so much the giving up of money, but he emphasizes that Ahaz gave up Judah's complete independence as well.

106. Boutflower, *The Book of Isaiah* (London: SPCK, 1930), pp. 49ff., sees Immanuel as Isaiah's third son (cf. too Hosea, who "also had three prophetic children"); Mueller, "A Virgin Shall Conceive," in *Evangelical Quarterly* XXXII (October, 1960): 203-207, accepts the RSV translation "maiden" and seeks to find the actual fulfillment of the prophecy in the birth of Maher-shalal-hash-baz or Hezekiah. For other speculations and a fuller discussion of this problem see the section on "Immanuel" above.

107. Machen, op. cit., pp. 290ff., says that Ahaz forfeited all claim to a sign and that since he was an unbeliever he could not understand the significance of the sign anyhow; Klingerman, *Messianic Prophecy in the Old Testament* (Grand Rapids: Zondervan, 1958), p. 75, says it applies to the Davidic line in specific and to the "whole human race" in general; Carroll, *The*

ever, one must guard against "overplaying" this tune. Many liberal and neo-orthodox theologians have dismissed the possibility of a predictive element in this passage simply on the grounds that the birth of Christ seven hundred years later could hardly mean anything to Ahaz.[108] Gray makes much of the necessity of a contemporary significance to Ahaz and maintains that the whole purpose of the sign is to bring a response of faith from Ahaz.[109] Therefore, he would need something more definite than a far-distant birth of a child. However, we must ask what was Ahaz's response? It was one of unbelief and rejection. Nowhere is there an indication that he heeded the prophet's warning.[110] For in the account in II Chronicles he proceeds to act against Isaiah's previous advice. Therefore, it is a very weak argument upon which to base one's interpretation of this passage. If the sign were to provoke such great faith from Ahaz, why did it fail? In referring to the idea that the child to be born could be any maiden's child, Cheyne asks of what significance would the birth of such an insignificant child be to Ahaz? He feels that Ahaz was "judicially hardened" and that his unbelief on this occasion was only a fresh degree of hardening.[111]

Even though the "sign" was given as a promise to the Davidic line and a warning to Judah, it is not necessary to eliminate Ahaz completely from the picture. It is necessary to determine the relation of the child's growth to the chronological development of events. Morgan maintains that the sign did have immediate significance to Ahaz in that he knew the enemy would be destroyed and that God would be with them in the person of Immanuel.[112] Orelli offers this explanation of the significance of the sign in relation to the development of the child:

> The sign consists primarily in this, that the rapid change impending over the land of Judah in the next years is revealed in the stages of a child's life. The child . . . will receive at his birth the name Immanuel, God with us, because just then, and so in a set

Prophets of the Assyrian Period (Nashville: Broadman, 1948), p. 108, says that the significance of the sign applies to the whole nation.

108. For an example see Mauchline, op. cit., pp. 98ff.
109. Gray, op. cit., p. 122ff.
110. For a good description of Ahaz, see Boutflower, op. cit., pp. 35-47.
111. Cheyne, op. cit., p. 49.
112. G. C. Morgan, op. cit., p. 47.

number of months, God's miraculous assistance will have been experienced. . . . But although in the formal exposition of the sign, the boy merely figures as an index of the fate of Judah, the significance of this child is not exhausted thereby . . . but contains the germ of a glorious future, in which the presence of Immanuel will ensure God's gracious help to his people. . . . Immanuel cannot be a mere hypothetical figure without real significance . . . on the contrary no other can be meant than the Messiah.[113]

Here then is the impact on Ahaz, on the royal line, and on the people of Jerusalem. In less time than it takes a child to discern right and wrong, destruction will come on their enemies, and eventually it will also come on them; but the line of David need not fear, for it will not become extinct. In fact, the coming Immanuel is so real in the prophet's conception that he sees the virgin as already pregnant. It is no wonder. With the sad state of affairs in Israel and Judah and the impending doom of both, Isaiah has realized that God must eventually intervene and establish His King, since the human rulers have failed so miserably.

Isaiah himself provides the interpretation of the sign. He states that the result of the coming invasion will be the frustration and elimination of the two hated kings (Rezin and Pekah) and that Israel will be destroyed so that within only one lifetime (65 years) she will no longer be a people. The ethnic strain of the nation will be eliminated. This is, of course, exactly what happened. A few years later Assyria carried off Ephraim captive and dispersed her children throughout the Mesopotamian area and re-populated her homeland with other captives from foreign lands. Thus developed the Samaritans, who were distinct from the "true Jews." As for the Northern Kingdom of Israel, it is even today often referred to as the "ten lost tribes." Certainly Isaiah meant what he said when he declared that they would "no longer be a people."

The message to Judah in the giving of the sign is connected with verses eight and nine. If Syria and Ephraim are destroyed and Judah still does not heed God, then she will not stand either. Therefore, despite the fact that Isaiah brings a message of hope in the present

---

113. Orelli, op. cit., pp. 56-57.

calamity, it is also a message of doom that is awaiting faithless Judah.[114]

The time element involved has always been a problem to interpreters. It is often asked how can so distant a fulfillment (in the birth of Christ) be related to these eighth-century events? Hengstenberg says that all messianic prophecies are distant, and Dewart asks, why not this one also?[115] Carroll says that the time element involved hinges on the term "before." He literally interprets the destruction of Damascus and Israel as being obviously before the growth of Jesus, since He is not yet born.[116] Whether or not this is an accurate interpretation, we can find a parallel situation in the Old Testament where a future event was a promise of less distant deliverance. In Exodus 3:12 the promise to Moses that Israel would worship at Mount Sinai was also a guarantee that they would first be delivered out of Egypt. The parallel is quite amazing. The Hebrews had to be released from Egypt before they could ever reach Sinai, and in Isaiah's time the throne of David had to be spared in order for the Messiah eventually to reign upon it.[117]

Even though this promise was delivered by God to His people, its full significance was understood only as the various aspects of it came into focus: the defeat of Rezin and Pekah; the disappearance of Israel; the eventual captivity of Judah; the coming of Immanuel. The emphasis of the "sign" was the hope that Immanuel would come and that a "remnant would return" from Judah's forthcoming defeat. The remnant (to whom chapters eight and nine are addressed) must return (not "disappear" as Israel will) so that the Messiah may come to the Davidic throne.[118]

---

114. Though presently spared, Judah too was finally defeated and taken captive to Babylon. Unlike Israel, though, Judah was promised that a remnant would return. Note the significance of Shear-yashub's presence with his father. For a contrary view see Mauchline, op. cit., p. 98. He interprets this passage as the destruction of Judah by Syria and Ephraim. Since this never fully happened, it is difficult to see the validity of such an interpretation.

115. See Dewart, op. cit., p. 125.

116. Carroll, op. cit., p. 108. He states that the text does not say "how long before," and that we have here an expression of the order of events rather than immediately successive sequence.

117. For a more complete discussion of this, see Alexander, op. cit., p. 119.

118. See previous discussion on the "Messiah in Prophecy."

The significance of a predicted virgin birth of the Messiah does have meaning to Ahaz. He will see Judah spared (however, by his alliances and not because of his trust in God), but he also, because of his lack of faith, will continue rolling Judah toward captivity, and he will not be established long as the ruler of Judah. Such graciousness of *Yahweh* to this ungodly ruler must be noted as a remarkable display of grace. This man, who brought a heathen altar into the temple, is privileged to receive a message of hope and a warning to turn from eventual destruction, and he rejects it. Therefore, the destruction must come, but yet there is hope for the house of David, for the virgin's son yet comes and He is God's "sign."[119] There is, therefore, both a message for the age and a message for the ages.

RELATIONSHIP OF ISAIAH 7:14 TO THE REST OF CHAPTERS 7–12

The main passage, however significant in its own right, must be considered in the entirety of its context. Dr. Culver warns, "Too often expositors have sought to explain one portion of the prophecy without the other."[120] In 7:14 we are given a very obscure reference to the birth of Immanuel, which is admittedly vague to the Old Testament man. However, when taken in the fullness of its context we have a much more definite picture, and we are given a better indication of how the New Testament interprets the single passage in 7:14.[121]

Assyrian Invasion

In chapter eight the prophet forthrightly proclaims the coming Assyrian invasion of the land. Though this is an admittedly difficult passage, its importance has been pointed to by Hengstenberg, who says it is intended to connect 7:14 to 9:6.[122] In verse eight we again

---

119. It is interesting to note Luke 2:25-35, where the godly Simeon refers to Jesus as a "sign"!

120. See his excellent discussion on the Immanuel prophecy in "Were the Old Testament Prophecies Really Prophetic?" in *Can I Trust My Bible?* (Chicago: Moody Press, 1963), p. 104.

121. Most agree with the division of the Immanuel passage as being chapters 7-12. See outline in Archer, op. cit., p. 314. Some maintain that chapters 7-9 though are one oracle, and 10-12 though connected are later. See Culver, ibid., p. 104.

122. Hengstenberg, *Christology*, vol. II, p. 49.

have a reference to "Immanu-el." This is preceded by the reference
to the birth of Isaiah's son, Maher-shalal-hash-baz.[123] The interpretation of the son is given by God Himself in verse four. He signifies
the invasion of Syria and Ephraim by Assyria, and thus he too is a
"sign" to Judah. The aspect of "hastening" in his name signifies the
quickly coming doom (as did the infancy of the new-born Immanuel
signify to the prophet's mind the hasty destruction of the northern
invaders).

The warning then is extended to Judah in verses 6-10.[124] The
nation is warned not to make an alliance with Assyria, for it will lead
to the invasion of Judah itself. In verse eight the prophet pictures
Assyria as a great river overflowing Judah, which is "thy land, O
Immanuel." Therefore, Immanuel is closely identified with the
land.[125] It is his land. Klausner sees this as a definite statement of
his royalty, as being the king of the land.[126] Finally, the prophet
restates his previous criticism of the national policy when he warns
that they are not to associate themselves with a foreign alliance for
the purpose of protection, for on the contrary they shall be "broken
in pieces" if they do so.

In verse ten he counters the question of their taking counsel with
a foreign pact, with the assurance that such is not necessary, for "God
is with us." Therefore, in chapter eight we are given more fully the
clear picture of Ahaz's part in this prophecy. His attitude of rejection
of God's "sign" officially represents the rejection by the entire nation. Thus we understand the significance of Isaiah's statement; it
not only is directed to Ahaz individually but to the whole nation
collectively. The monarch's disobedience only typifies that of the
entire nation. Judah will not heed the counsel of God, or accept

---

123. This has led many to connect both names to the same individual in
asserting that Immanuel is the prophet's son (see previous sections).

124. Notice the similarity to chapter 7. In both passages (7:8-9 and 8:4-8)
Assyria is to destroy Syria and Ephraim and then turn on faithless Judah.

125. Hengstenberg, op. cit., p. 49, takes the significance of this passage to
be a promise that the land in which Immanuel is to be born is not to remain
the property of heathen enemies.

126. Klausner, op. cit., pp. 56-57. Though he argues that Immanuel is
Hezekiah, he, nevertheless, gives a good statement of reasons as to why this
passage has a messianic ruler of Judah in mind.

His sign, therefore God gives to the nation a sign of judgment and hope. The object of judgment is Judah's willful disobedience and faithlessness. The source of hope is God's merciful intention of bringing His ruler to the throne which He had promised to David as "a throne forever."

The Child in Chapter Nine

Chapter nine culminates this promise of hope in a coming ruler: the "gift-child." This passage provides the conclusion of the oracle begun in chapter seven and sheds further light on who Immanuel is to be.[127] The full statement, then, is of both Immanuel's human birth and divine origin. Delitzsch sees this "gift-child" as the same person who is the virgin's son. Contrasted to the Syrian-Ephraimitic coalition, a Child brings deliverance to the people of God. Again the emphasis of the passage, as in 7:14, falls upon the Child.[128] And again the prophet speaks of him as though he were already born.

The perfect tense of the verb emphasizes the actual historicity of this birth. If this birth is to bring blessing to God's people, it must be an actual event at a definite time and in a definite place. The promise of eternal sovereignty had been connected to the throne of David since the declaration in II Samuel 7.[129] Also the messianic concept of One who is both the Son of David and the Son of God (Ps. 2:7) was not a new one at this time.[130] It is quite possible, therefore, that this passage is a clear prediction of the divine Messiah.

The four titles of the child are obviously significant, but have received wide comment. Klausner and Luzzatto see the entire phrase as one gigantic title.[131] Klausner translates Isaiah 9:6 as: "And his name shall be called: Wonderful in counsel is God the Mighty,

---

127. Culver, op. cit., p. 104, states that, "In context it is most difficult to prove that the virgin's son has any connection at all with Mary's babe unless one continues on to the final verses of the prophecy. . . ."

128. See E. Young, *Commentary,* vol. I, p. 329, for a lengthy discussion of the grammatical structure of this passage and its significance upon interpreting the child's identity.

129. See discussion in Delitzsch, op. cit., p. 248.

130. The text of the Targum also supports a messianic interpretation of this passage. See Stenning, op. cit., p. 62.

131. Dillmann remarked that this would be an "unparalleled monstrosity." Op. cit., p. 251.

the Everlasting Father, the Ruler of peace."[132] Such a lenghty name,
however, is unparalleled in Scripture. Also the use of the disjunctive
accent *telisha* at the head of the statement would not give the type of
separation required here.[133] The force of the *zakeph* subordinates
all the words from ויקרא onwards, so that the distribution would be:
ויקרא שמו פלא יועץ אל גבור אבי־עד שר־שלום. Young points
out that the Masoretic accentuation supports the concept of four
names. He states that in the four names "a remarkable symmetry
is obtained. Each name consists of two members, and each half of
the verse of two names.[134] He also follows Herntrich in affirming that
each doublet emphasizes the Child's humanity and His deity. Thus:

    PELE yoetz EL gibbor   abi AD   sar SHALOM

    Others do not deny a messianic reference here, but see the four
titles as dependently based upon the formal Egyptian titulary.[135]
This seems quite erroneous for several reasons. Isaiah 9:6 has four
titles and the Egyptian titulary has five. Also, the Egyptian titulary is
very specialized, reflecting distinct throne and deity names. Such is
not at all the usage in Isaiah, nor is there any indication that a Hebrew king ever used such a title.[136] Rather, the Hebrew titles form
a series of epithets which are stylistically much closer to the Ugaritic
literature than is the rather specialized titulary of the pharaohs.[137]

---

   132. Klausner, op. cit., p. 64.
   133. The *telisha* in פלא is the smallest of all disjunctive accents; the *geresh*
in שמו is stronger, and the *pashta* in יועץ is stronger than both of them; but
the *zakeph* in גבור is the greatest divider in the sentence. For the best detailed discussion of the usage of accents in this passage see Delitzsch, op. cit.,
p. 250.
   134. E. Young, *Commentary*, p. 333.
   135. For example, von Rad, *"Das judaische Königsritual"* in *Theologische
Literaturzeitung* 72 (1942), cols. 215-216, argues that such a dependence here
illustrates the Hebrew dependence upon Egyptian influence in their kingship
concept, so that even the Messiah reflects the Egyptian model. Following this
precedent, Alt, *Kleine Schriften*, II, pp. 219ff., tried to emend the verse to
produce five titles to correspond with the Egyptian usage.
   136. For the most scholarly criticism of the concept that Hebrew kingship
was based on the Egyptian model, see Kitchen, *Ancient Orient and Old Testament* (Chicago: InterVarsity Press, 1966), pp. 106-11.
   137. See Kitchen, ibid., p. 110, for evidence of a Semitic parallel to a
broken tablet from North-Canaanite Ugarit which gives a series of epithets to
Niqmepa, which describe him as a "Lord of justice," "master of the (royal)
house," "protector," and "builder."

Similarly, these four titles in Isaiah are actually descriptions of the ruler.

Wonderful Counsellor. Isaiah introduces the Child as not only wonderful, but is Himself a wonder (cf. Judges 13:18, where God is called a "wonder," passing human thought and power). יוֹעֵץ is an appositional genitive to פֶּלֶא and may be rendered "a wonder of a counsellor" or "a wonderful counsellor."[138] The term *counsellor* is often used in parallel with *king* (e.g., Micah 4:9), so that the emphasis here is implying that this Child gives God-like counsel and is a God-like King.

Mighty God. This key title has been one of the most disputed in the passage.[139] In Isaiah, *el* is always used of God and never refers to a man. In 10:21 he says that a remnant of Jacob will return to *el gibbor*. This usage of *el gibbor* for God is also paralleled in Ugaritic literature.[140] Also, the easy transition between gods and men that is so common in pagan literature is completely foreign to the Old Testament, so that it is highly certain that the reference here is to God Himself. *Gibbor* means "hero." If it is an appositional genitive, the rendering would be, "a god of a hero"; if it be used adjectivally, it would be "a heroic god." In either case the descriptive epithet indicates divinity. There is, therefore, every indication that this Child is to be the "Mighty God" Himself. Such revelation explains how the child in 7:14 could be born of a virgin.

Eternal Father. This aspect even more clearly affixes deity to the Child; He is none other than God Himself. The expression אֲבִי־עַד is a peculiar way to express "everlasting" and literally indicates "father of eternity."[141] He is the lord of eternity as well as the author of eternal life. He is "from old, from everlasting," and He is a father to His people. "Thou, O Lord, art our father, and our

---

138. E. Young, *Commentary*, p. 334. He states that such counseling is given by God (cf. Ps. 16:7; 32:8; Prov. 1:30; 8:14).

139. G. A. Smith, op. cit., p. 135, hesitates to understand any reference to God by these names and sees only a "God-Hero," who appears to be an *el* to his people.

140. See references and discussion in E. Young, *Commentary*, p. 336.

141. Archer, *W.B.C.*, op. cit., p. 619, provides an excellent discussion of verse 6. He points out that all five occurrences of *el gibbor* in the Old Testament refer to God.

redeemer; thy name is from everlasting" (Isa. 63:16). He is the
fatherly shepherd who guards His children, and there is no end to
His kingdom. Here we are told how the throne of David, which is
to be forever, is to be preserved. It will seat a Ruler who Himself
is eternal.

Prince of Peace. His reign is to be characterized by a rule of
peace on earth. Rather than a warring monarch, He who is the
Mighty God will be a benevolent Father bringing peace which will
also be eternally established.[142] He will be the very embodiment of
peace.

In referring to the context of chapters seven through nine, Baron
states that no longer is the unidentified Immanuel obscure as in
7:14. For now we know His human birth; throne (of David); the
extent of His reign (to all nations); the peaceful character of this
reign; the eternal duration of it.[143] More than this we know who He
is. He is God Himself in the form of a man. Also, we know how it
is possible for the "virgin" to be a virgin and yet at the same time
be pregnant ("therefore that holy thing which shall be born to you
shall be called the Son of God"—Luke 1:35).

A Shoot from the Stump

The time of the Messiah's coming was undoubtedly a great puzzle
to the Old Testament man. Isaiah's prophecies in chapters seven
through nine indicate that Immanuel, the virgin-born, divine Child,
is soon to come. However, in chapter eleven we see the proper sequence of events at His coming is definitely moved into the future,
since the tree of David has been cut down, and the shoot must grow
out of the rootstock of Jesse before the tree can flourish again.
Isaiah's point is to show that the kingdom has sunk so low that the
very Davidic line, whose perpetuity was the matter of Ahaz's concern, will actually be cut down. So hopeless is the present condition
that it is necessary to begin anew. The prophet sees the mighty
dynasty of David as only a felled tree; all that remains is the עֵץ

---

142. E. Young, *Commentary,* pp. 339-40, says this "includes more than a
temporary cessation of hostilities. . . . He removed the cause of war, namely,
human sin."

143. Baron, op. cit., p. 32.

"rootstock," "stump." (See Job 14:8 and Isa. 40:24, where it is the stump of a fallen tree.) From the stump a twig would sprout (יצא) and from the roots a branch would flourish again. That flourishing will accomplish the true purpose of God through David's throne, for it will bring righteousness and faithfulness and the destruction of the wicked (vss. 4-5).

In verse two this "shoot" is personalized as an individual ruler. The Spirit of the Lord will be upon Him and give Him wisdom, perception, counsel, might, knowledge, fear of the Lord. How close the parallel is to chapter nine! Verse four extends His influence over all the earth. He will judge the oppressed of earth; rule with a rod of iron; and slay the wicked with the breath of His mouth. Such statements, such glorious aspirations have never been applied to any human ruler in Judah.

Viewing the entire context of the Immanuel passage, we are told that the throne of David need not fear threatening, for "God is with us" in the birth of the virgin's Son. Then we are told that He is to be identified with the land; it is His land. Next, He is described as a gift-Child who assumes the government. Further, we are told that He is Himself the Mighty God, the Everlasting Father, whose role will bring peace through His wonderful counsel. Immanuel is to be God Himself born of a virgin into human flesh in the capacity of the Messiah who is to rule over all the earth. Finally, we are told that before He comes the tree of David will be reduced to a stump. Judah need not fear, for the time will yet come when God's King will sit on the throne. When the branch sprouts from the stock of Jesse, it will be to an eternal reign. All the indications of this context point to the coming of Jesus Christ. In particular the 7:14 passage seems to point to His coming in the virgin birth. How can we be certain what Isaiah meant? What did the earliest interpreters of this passage say that he meant?

Chapter Four

EARLY INTERPRETATION OF ISAIAH 7:14

REFERENCE IN MICAH

The messianic passage in Micah 5:2 has long been applied to the birth of the Messiah, who would be a "son of David." Much discussion has been prompted over the reference in verse three to "she which travaileth." It has been said that herein is a reference by Isaiah's contemporary to the same pregnant virgin as is mentioned in Isaiah 7:14.[1] If this be true, we have the earliest possible reference to Isaiah's prophecy, by one of his own contemporaries.[2] Despite the brevity of his writing, the message which he proclaimed reached a society "guilty of social crimes and personal sin."[3]

The context containing the reference to "she that travaileth" is one of the promised glory to the Davidic line.[4] The armies of Judah are

1. N. Snaith, *Amos, Hosea and Micah* (London: Epworth Press, 1960), p. 95. This eminent Jewish scholar definitely believes Micah 5:3 to be a reference to Isaiah 7:14-16, though, of course, he denies that either applies to Christ, except as the Christian church has forced the meaning. Nevertheless, he gives good support to the fact of a direct relation between the statements of Micah and Isaiah.

2. The prophet Micah was a citizen of Moresheth-Gath, a town in the foothills on the edge of the Philistine Plain, which formed a fertile agricultural valley. He was a prophet to Judah, and Jerusalem in particular, during the reigns of Jotham, Ahaz, and Hezekiah. Little is known of him personally, but the prophet Jeremiah (26:18) gives worthy tribute to his remarkable influence as a preacher. For a good discussion of the prophet and an introduction to his book see J. S. Baxter, *Explore the Book* (Grand Rapids: Zondervan, 1962), vol. IV, pp. 187-94, and S. Schultz, *The Old Testament Speaks* (New York: Harper & Row, 1960), pp. 395-99.

3. J. Marsh, *Amos and Micah* (London: SCM Press, 1959), p. 83.

4. The text of Micah is quite well established. There has been some wide disagreement on possible additions to the original, but none have been well established. See Cheyne, *Micah* (Cambridge: University Press, 1909), p. 44. He says 4:1–5:14 could be late. On the other hand Sellin took chapters 4–5 as a pre-exilic appendage to a later main body! See discussion of Sellin's view in G. L. Robinson, *The Twelve Minor Prophets* (New York: R. Smith Inc., 1930), p. 185.

to prepare against a siege by Assyria, yet the little village of Bethlehem Ephratah is given the promise that one would come forth to be a ruler in Israel. Bethlehem is, of course, the city of Jesse, from which David originally came. However, all ensuing generations of . monarchs came from Jerusalem, the capital city. This is an unprecedented figure to use for the seat of rulership, the village where David was born.

Also, note that this ruler's "goings forth" are "from old, from everlasting." This qualification seems to be more personal to the individual than it does apply to the Davidic dynasty.[5] Micah proceeds to proclaim that Israel will be "given up" until the time when "she which travaileth hath brought forth." Interestingly he places the condition of pregnancy (here, travailing) in the present sense as does Isaiah. Lowth maintained that "this prophecy obviously and plainly refers to some known prophecy concerning a woman who is to bring forth a child." He concludes that this "seems more properly applicable to this passage of Isaiah, than to any others."[6] Since Micah does not say he is quoting from Isaiah, we cannot be positively certain that he is. However, he does at times make very clear reference to what Isaiah has already proclaimed, and, since they were contemporary to Ahaz's time as prophets in Jerusalem, there is little doubt that he was aware of what sign Isaiah had given to the king. Chances are good that they even discussed it at a later time. It is difficult to deny that Micah, having a personal awareness of Isaiah's preaching, does refer to the same prophecy as given earlier by the senior prophet.[7]

---

5. Even Snaith, op. cit., p. 95, agrees that this is a reference to the birth of a great king at Bethlehem who would be of unusual qualities and would be heir to the throne of David.

6. Lowth, op. cit., p. 231. He reasons that since Micah refers to the Isaiah 7:14 prophecy, it must have been well known. He also gives a good discussion (p. 230) on Micah's use of statements previously made by Isaiah.

7. Marsh, op. cit., p. 115, does deny it, but offers no substantiation for his action. Meanwhile, most commentators cannot escape the fact that all indications point to Micah's reference as a quotation of Isaiah. Cheyne, op. cit., pp. 45-46, says despite doubts Micah 5:3 and Isaiah 7:14 are complementary references to the Messiah. He also takes 5:5 ("this man shall be peace") as a reference to Isaiah 9:6. Snaith, op. cit., p. 95, offers no hesitation that Micah is quoting from Isaiah. G. C. Morgan, op. cit., takes Micah's reference

If, therefore, Micah did in all probability quote Isaiah, we may determine from Micah's usage what his interpretation of Isaiah was. Here, he is clearly presenting the birthplace of the Messiah, the Davidic ruler. In the time of Herod there was no question to the scribes that Micah was speaking of the birth of the Messiah at Bethlehem. Their viewpoint gives us one of the clearest statements of early rabbinical interpretation of Micah.[8] The significance of this passage should not be underestimated. For most critics have denied its messianic intention, saying that it only signifies a ruler coming from the line of David, and that Bethlehem is merely a symbolic literary device and has no real reference to his actual birthplace.[9] Yet, the scholars of Herod's time took this to be, in fact, a prediction of his birthplace. Herod did not send his soldiers to Jerusalem to slaughter the male children. He sent them to Bethlehem. Every indication in Matthew's record is that everyone involved—Herod, the scribes, and the magi—all accepted a literal interpretation of the passage.

If Micah, then, is quoting from Isaiah, and also in this section is referring to the birthplace of the coming Messiah, we may conclude with the highest degree of probability that he is interpreting Isaiah 7:14 as a reference to the birth of the Messiah.[10] Therefore, as Robinson has well stated, Isaiah tells of the Christ's "virgin birth," and Micah of His "village birth."[11] It is true that יוֹלֵדָה does not necessarily indicate present time itself, but the reference to "the time she has brought forth" does indicate that, though she is "giving birth," she has not yet borne this one who will stand in the strength and majesty of the Lord. In figure the nation travails in bringing forth

---

as conclusive evidence that Isaiah 7:14 is a prediction of the birth of Messiah. Copass and Carlson, *A Study of the Prophet Micah* (Grand Rapids: Baker, 1950), p. 129, also agree.

8. See the excellent comments and evidence given by G. Robinson, op. cit., p. 98, and C. Feinberg, *Jonah, Micah, Nahum* (New York: American Missions to the Jews, 1951), p. 95.

9. For an example see Marsh, op. cit., pp. 114-115.

10. It is interesting to note that Micah regards the pregnancy of the woman as still impending and not yet completed. If this reference is a quotation of Isaiah's prophecy, it tends to argue against those who assert that the child in Isaiah 7:14 is about to be born within a few months.

11. Robinson, loc. cit., p. 98.

a great ruler, but in fact it is God who brings forth His Ruler through the matronage of Miriam of Nazareth. He is to be born in Bethlehem, the town where David himself was born. Since no other Jewish king was born there since David's time, we can conclude that only Jesus Christ fits the fulfillment of this passage. More pertinently to the present study, we may also conclude that Micah does possibly give us the earliest messianic interpretation of Isaiah 7:14. There is at least a great deal of similarity between the two passages, though perhaps not enough to be conclusive.

TRANSLATION OF THE SEPTUAGINT

The Septuagint is the first and foremost ancient translation of the Hebrew Old Testament into Greek. It was compiled in Egypt during the second and third centuries B.C. It most likely arose to meet the need of the Greek-speaking Jews of Alexandria. It represents a collection of translations of the Old Testament produced by Jews of the Diaspora.[12] It came to have wide usage among Greek-speaking Jews and later was often quoted by the Christian church. It is a valuable witness to the understanding of the Old Testament in the pre-Christian era, since its translations represent an interpretation as well as a philological work.

It is, therefore, significant that the LXX[13] uses the Greek word παρθένος to translate the word עַלְמָה in Isaiah 7:14.[14] Παρθένος is used in Greek to mean "virgin."[15] Either the translators felt that the עַלְמָה of Isaiah was grammatically meant to precisely indicate a "virgin," or they so interpreted Isaiah's usage of the term to mean a "virgin." Probably the grammatical aspect is true, since the LXX generally uses παρθένος for עַלְמָה. In either case, however, we are

---

12. For a good discussion of the compilation and disunity of the LXX, see article on "Septuagint" by J. Graybill in *Zondervan Pictorial Bible Dictionary* (Grand Rapids: Zondervan, 1963), pp. 770-71.

13. The Septuagint is designated LXX because it was supposedly the work of seventy scholars.

14. The general usage in the LXX of παρθένος is for designating both בתולה and עלמה.

15. Arndt and Gingrich, op. cit., p. 632, concur that from earliest usage (Homer, inscriptions, papyri, and LXX) παρθένος is to be rendered as "virgin." They also point to this usage after הָעַלְמָה הָרָה in Isaiah 7:14.

given a very clear position by a very early source. To the LXX there is no doubt that Isaiah intended '*almah* to mean "virgin," and, therefore, the LXX indicates an acceptance of the virgin birth concept of the Messiah as prevalent at that time.

VIEW OF THE QUMRAN LITERATURE

The use of παρθένος for עַלְמָה is also reflected in material from the Dead Sea Scrolls.[16] This pre-Christian material antedates previous Old Testament copies by nearly one thousand years and is of tremendous importance to biblical studies in confirming the authenticity of the Hebrew Bible.[17]

Also, the concept of the virgin birth itself is reflected in this material. The thanksgiving psalm 1 Q H iii refers to the coming virgin birth of the Branch.[18] However, not all scholars are convinced of the reference.[19] For our purposes the best evidence from the scrolls is the consistent usage of παρθένος in Greek material to refer to '*almah*. Thus, we have a very ancient authority to support the assertion that '*almah* is most naturally to be translated as "virgin."[20] There is ample support, then, for the grammatical usage of '*almah*. What of the theological concept of a virgin-born Messiah? For an adequate answer the writings of the Jewish theologians of this period must be considered.

INTERPRETATION OF RABBINIC TEACHING

The consideration of rabbinic theology of the pre-Christian era on the subject of the virgin birth and on the interpretation of Isaiah 7:14 has not been given thorough consideration by most writers.

---

16. Knight, op. cit., p. 310, concludes that it is difficult to escape the fact that all indications in the Qumran scrolls seem to interpret '*almah* as "virgin."

17. For a scholarly, concise, and well-organized approach to the Qumran literature see M. Mansoor, *The Dead Sea Scrolls* (Grand Rapids: Eerdmans, 1964).

18. See discussion by R. Gordis, "The 'Begotten' Messiah in the Qumran Scrolls," *Vetus Testamentum* VII (April, 1957): 191ff.

19. Mansoor, loc. cit., pp. 103-4, says such a reference is not clear in the "wondrous counselor" who is brought forth.

20. See the evidence on the use of "virgin" in the Dead Sea Scrolls given by C. T. Fritsch, *The Qumran Community* (1956), p. 35.

Yet, if there is significant evidence that the concept of a virgin-born Messiah existed among these writers, we would obviously be able to conclude that they must have acquired such a concept from some place, and that Isaiah would be the most likely source from whom they developed their ideas.

First, consider the concept of a virgin-born Messiah. Skinner provides a good history of pre-Christian Jewish interpretation of this concept.[21] He states that the Jews developed an eschatological hope in a personal Messiah that surpassed contemporary circumstances.[22] He shows that they regarded Micah 5:3 and the LXX quotations as the earliest trace of the acceptance of a virgin birth prediction which came to prevail among most Alexandrian and some Palestinian Jews.[23] Skinner concludes that only after the Christians accepted the Old Testament virgin-birth passages as referring to Jesus did the Jews change their interpretation of the Messiah in the Old Testament. Also, as previously noted, the scribes' interpretation in Herod's time reflects the contemporary rabbinic interpretation of a personal Messiah in the Old Testament.

Secondly, and more importantly, is the rabbinic interpretation of the exact passage under consideration. In this respect another converted Jew, Edersheim, has provided an excellent tracing of this material.[24] He shows that both the Isaiah 7:14 and the Micah 5:3 reference are messianically supported in the Talmud. The Jewish

---

21. Skinner, op. cit., pp. 63-64, lists several sources that provide excellent evidence for pre-Christian virgin birth interpretation of Isaiah 7:14.

22. Many modern day writers would not agree. The first to deny a personal Messiah seems to have been Hillel in the first century A.D. He said: "There is no Messiah for Israel, for they have already enjoyed him in the days of Hezekiah" (Sanhedrin XCVIII. col. 2). Yet even later rabbis, including such well-known teachers as Aben Ezra (1088–1176), Rashi Solomon Isaaki (1040–1095), Rabbi David Kimchi (1160–1235), Abarbanel Ben Jehudah (1437–1508) agreed that the O.T. teaches a personal Messiah. See the excellent discussion by the Hebrew Christian, D. Baron, *Rays of Messiah's Glory* (Grand Rapids: Zondervan, n.d.), pp. 16-20. He quotes Abarbanel (p. 19) as saying: "Whoever doubts that [i.e., that Messiah will come] makes the law to lie . . . and denies God and the words of his prophets."

23. See discussion and evidence by F. P. Badhams in his article in the *Academy*, June 8, 1895.

24. A. Edersheim, *The Life and Times of Jesus the Messiah* (Grand Rapids: Eerdmans, 1962), vol. II, pp. 723, 735.

writer, Greenstone, states that the Talmud reflects a concept of a divine Messiah with supernatural qualities and deeds.[25] He sees the rabbinic interpretation of Isaiah 7:14 as a "development of the ideal of the Messiah child."[26] He also finds reference to the birth of Messiah in the apocalyptic book of Zerubabel.[27]

Throughout the Gospels we are told that the common Jewish attitude of the day was that of messianic anticipation. Since Matthew wrote his εὐαγγέλιον as a "bridge" between the Old and New Covenants and especially showed from the Old Testament that Jesus was the Messiah, it is highly probable that his use of the Isaiah 7:14 quotation was implemented to find ready acceptance by the general populace. If the LXX, Qumran scrolls, and some of the early rabbinic commentators saw Isaiah 7:14 as a virgin-birth prediction, then Matthew had every historical precedent for the usage he gave the passage. The bulk of historical evidence supports an inter-testamental-period view of Isaiah's prediction of a virgin-born Messiah. This evidence is the best early support of a messianic interpretation of Isaiah 7:14 apart from any "fulfillment" in a contemporary event.

QUOTATION BY MATTHEW

In the first Gospel of the New Testament Matthew has compiled a record of the life and ministry of Christ that forms a "bridge" to the Hebrew Scriptures. More than any other gospel chronicles he quotes from the Old Testament and relates its theology, law, and prophecy to the events of Christ's life. In 1:23 we find a quotation of Isaiah 7:14. The text reads, "Behold, the virgin shall be with child, and shall bear a Son, and they shall call His name Immanuel; which translated means, God with us."[28] The context is the visit of

---

25. J. Greenstone, *The Messianic Idea in Jewish History* (Philadelphia: Jewish Publication Society of America, 1943), p. 109.

26. Ibid., pp. 33ff., provides a good discussion on sources of the virgin-born Messiah concept in pre-Christian Judaism. He personally feels that Isaiah hoped for the Messiah in the birth of Hezekiah and later, realizing he was not, penned chapter 11 as a distant future reference to him.

27. Ibid., p. 135. He discusses the reference to the "mother of Messiah": *Hephzibah* ("my desire is in her"), pointing to the early interpretation of "desire of nations" as being the Messiah.

28. *New American Standard Bible—New Testament* (Chicago: Moody Press, 1963).

the angel to Joseph to reassure him that Mary's condition of pregnancy is a conception "of the Holy Spirit," obviously implying that it is not the result of adultery.[29] The indication is also presented here that there is, therefore, no human father involved in this birth. Joseph is told that the child will be a boy and is to be named Jesus, "for it is He who will save His people from their sins." Next comes the quotation from Isaiah prefixed by the statement, "Now all this has taken (marg.) place that what was spoken by the Lord through the prophet might be fulfilled" (vs. 22). Awaking from his sleep, Joseph did as commanded and married Mary and "kept her a virgin until she gave birth to a son; and he called his name Jesus" (vs. 25).

It is hardly necessary to state that this passage is of greatest significance in determining the identity of Immanuel. One cannot deny the authority of the text. It states that Isaiah had predicted the birth of Jesus. If Isaiah did not intend Immanuel to be the Messiah, then where did Matthew get the authority to make such a statement? The question presupposes one of three possible answers: (1) Isaiah did mean to refer to Christ and Matthew's account is the true interpretation. (2) Isaiah did not so intend and Matthew, therefore, must be wrong in what he says. (3) Isaiah did not directly refer to Christ but Matthew saw through inspiration a further development that he applied to Him. Prophecy was to prepare for the coming of Christ so clearly that His coming would be recognized as a fulfillment of such prophecy when compared to it.[30] Either this passage was clear to Matthew or else it was not.[31] There have been those who think Mat-

---

29. G. Cox, *The Gospel According to St. Matthew* (London: SCM Press, 1956), pp. 29-30. This writer apparently is not as convinced by the angel's report as Joseph was, for he says of Joseph: "But whether she was an adulteress or a chosen vessel of God, she was no longer to be his. . . . His delicate scrupulosity is, however, overcome by an angelic reassurance, and Mary becomes his wife. . . . These words do no more than affirm that Jesus was not the natural son of Joseph." His obvious insinuation is that he was some other man's son! He admits the appearance of the angel (a supernatural event) but denies the virgin birth on the mere basis that Matthew quoted from the LXX.

30. See again Hengstenberg, op. cit., IV, p. 238.

31. Stendahl of Harvard, in *The School of St. Matthew* (Uppsala, 1954), pp. 98, 199, feels that parts of Matthew 1:18-25 may be alien portions later grafted into the text to supplement the genealogy, but he definitely states that rendering of *'almah* as *parthenos* (in 1:23) follows the LXX and is not a late Christian interpolation.

thew was not correct in what he was doing.[32] Probably a more comfortable critical position is to attempt to retain Matthew's intent but reject his method. The viewpoint of the *Interpreter's Bible* is illustrative of the general approach of this viewpoint:

> The quote from Matthew 1:23 is taken from the LXX, not from the Hebrew, and is one of a number of such quotations used by the author of that Gospel to show that the Old Testament foreshadowed the life of Jesus Christ. That he used these without particular regard to their meaning in their original context is clear . . . this latter "messianic interpretation" is derived from the conviction that the messianic hope had been fulfilled in Jesus. This conviction we may firmly retain, while recognizing that the New Testament's use of Isaiah 7:14 is based on an inaccurate translation of the Hebrew text, which must not prejudice our interpretation of this verse in its original setting.[33]

These same basic arguments are presented by Filson, Hamilton, and Cox.[34] Cox has previously been mentioned in this section. Filson is quite interesting. He maintains that Matthew's usage of the genealogy and the fulfillment of prophecy are both "God's working," yet he denies that Isaiah meant the virgin birth of Christ and that Matthew finds here a "parallel" to the life of Christ."[35] Hamilton of Colgate-Rochester Divinity School is also interesting. Now a leading exponent of the Theothanatology ("God is dead") movement, it hardly seems logical that he could be the author of such a non-secular work as a commentary on the Gospels. Writing in 1959, he does not deny the virgin birth itself, only that Isaiah predicted it.[36]

---

32. Many feel that Matthew was mistaken. See Driver, op. cit., p. 40, and Argyle, *The Gospel According to Matthew* (Cambridge: University Press, 1963), p. 28.

33. *Interpreter's Bible* (New York: Abingdon), vol. V, p. 218. It is interesting to note that the exegetical and homiletical sections of this work are done by different authors, and on the same page the exegete denies Isaiah is predicting the birth of Christ, and the expositor says to preach that this is the virgin birth! See note 46 in chapter 3.

34. F. Filson, *A Commentary on the Gospel According to St. Matthew* (New York: Harper and Row, 1961), pp. 54-55. W. Hamilton, *Modern Reader's Guide to Matthew and Luke* (New York: Association Press, 1959), pp. 20-21. G. Cox, op. cit., pp. 29-30.

35. Filson in ibid., pp. 54-55.

36. Hamilton, op. cit., pp. 20-21. He feels that it was the church that later mis-applied Isaiah 7:14.

How different an attitude from that which he expresses in 1966, when he (with Altizer) affirms that "radical theology must finally understand the Incarnation itself as effecting the death of God."[37]

Held has taken a different approach toward Matthew's compilation.[38] He proposes that Matthew composed the birth story himself using a narrating technique involving the implementation of "catchwords":

> By the notion of linkage by catchwords is generally meant the technique of putting together different units of the tradition which are independent of each other, above all the sayings, on the basis of a common catchword.[39]

Whether this observation is of any significance remains to be demonstrated. Held makes no real point of the issue. It is obvious that some words would be repeated, since Matthew talks of the naming of Immanuel and the naming of Jesus. To assert, however, that the instruction of the angel to "call his name Jesus" and the reference to the virgin "calling his name Immanuel" and the actual naming of Jesus are connecting unrelated patches of the nativity story remains to be seen. How else was he supposed to relate these instances? Naturally he would use similar phraseology. This usage, while an interesting observation, could just as easily show the unity of relationship in the account as it is supposed to display the connection arbitrarily given to what was originally a disunity. There are other key matters that will shed greater light on this passage.

Usage of παρθένος

It has previously been noted (see above, note 31) that nearly

---

37. T. Altizer and W. Hamilton, *Radical Theology and the Death of God* (Indianapolis: Bobbs-Merrill, 1966), p. xii. For an excellent critique of this movement, its leaders, and its anti-theology see J. W. Montgomery, *The 'Is God Dead?' Controversy* (Grand Rapids: Zondervan, 1966).

38. Which he borrowed from Bultmann, *The History of the Synoptic Tradition* (Oxford, 1963).

39. G. Bornkamm, G. Barth, and H. Held, *Tradition and Interpretation in Matthew* (Philadelphia: Westminster, 1963), pp. 238-39. Held gives this list of "catchwords": 1:20/24 παραλαβεῖν τὴν γυναῖκα, 1:21/23/25 τίκτειν υἱόν, 1:21/23/25 χαλεῖν τὸ ὄνομα αὐτοῦ.

all contemporary commentators maintain that Matthew's usage of παρθένος in place of 'almah in the quotation of Isaiah 7:14 reflects a translation of the Septuagint (Greek Old Testament, translated in the third century B.C.). The insinuation is that the Septuagint gives a wrong translation and that Matthew, therefore, is mistaken in his usage. The reason for this criticism of Matthew is the argument over the Hebrew term 'almah, which many feel should not be rendered "virgin" (see discussion above in the section on "Almah"). Yet the Greek term παρθένος is always to be interpreted "virgin."[40] The question here is whether the LXX is wrong in its usage of παρθένος. Since this word was used by its translators to reflect the proper translation of 'almah, we must at least conclude that this is the opinion of this ancient authority. Therefore in c. 200 B.C. it was obviously felt that Isaiah was referring to a virgin (see previous discussions on "Almah" and the "Septuagint"). It is, then, unfair to conclude any more than that Matthew is inaccurate in following a historic precedent.[41] If 'almah can possibly be translated "virgin," and if this was the interpretation of most ancient authorities (Micah, LXX, and some Jewish rabbis), it is most likely then that Matthew is correct in his usage of παρθένος. Bishop Lowth (a critic of the unity of Isaiac authorship) wrote in the early nineteenth century:

> St. Matthew therefore in applying this prophecy to the birth of Christ does it not merely in the way of accommodating the words . . . but takes it in its strictest, clearest, and most important sense and applies it according to the original and principal intention of the prophet.[42]

Usage of ἵνα

In his statement that this passage from Isaiah is "fulfilled" in Jesus, Matthew indicates, then, that Isaiah was in fact predicting the virgin birth of Christ. The term πληρωθῇ is preceded by the important little word ἵνα. Since Matthew appears to use the phrase, "that it might be fulfilled," in different ways, it is necessary to de-

---

40. Arndt and Gingrich, op. cit., p. 632.
41. So concludes E. Rogers, *Jesus the Christ: A Survey of Matthew's Gospel* (London: Pickering and Inglis, 1962), p. 19.
42. Lowth, op. cit., p. 231.

termine whether he saw in Isaiah a definite prediction or merely a corresponding parallel.[43] The phrase ἵνα πληρωθῇ indicates complete fulfillment but not always direct prediction (e.g., Matt. 2:15, 18). However, this still does not indicate a double fulfillment in two separately intended events.[44] It is quite possible, then, that Matthew saw Isaiah's prophecy as completely fulfilled in the one event: the birth of Christ.

Usage of πληρωθῇ

Matthew's usage of this word (1:22) indicates that he definitely saw a predictive fulfillment of Isaiah's prophecy in Christ. This form, "to fulfill," is found frequently throughout the first Gospel.[45] Broadus states that the usual meaning implies real prediction.[46] Lenski adds: "The verb πληρωθῇ pictures the promise or prophecy as an empty vessel which is at last filled when the event occurs."[47] The crux of the matter, though, is its usage in this particular context. Arndt and Gingrich render the usage of πληρωθῇ in Matthew 1:22 as "the fulfillment of divine prediction or promise."[48] There can be no doubt, then, that Matthew firmly believed this reference in Isaiah was definitely a prediction of an event that was filled to the full in Jesus' birth. One wishing to deny the predictive element of Isaiah or its acceptance by the early church cannot adequately do it on a philological-grammatical basis, nor on the basis of historical precedent.

---

43. This phraseology can take various aspects. Rogers, op. cit., p. 17, points out that ὅυτως used with πληρωθῇ indicates a partial fulfillment and that with τότε merely an illustration of a prophecy. Stonehouse, *The Witness of Matthew and Mark to Christ* (London: Lutterworth, 1944), p. 126, shows that Matthew uses the form τότε over ninety times.

44. For a good discussion of the New Testament usage of the word and the Old Testament implications of prophecy by "type" or "extension" see the article by R. Culver, "The Old Testament as Messianic Prophecy," in *Bulletin of the Evangelical Theological Society* 7 (Summer, 1964): 91-97.

45. See vss. 1:22; 2:15, 17, 23; 4:14; 8:17; 12:17; 13:35; 21:4; 26:54, 56; 27:9.

46. J. Broadus, *Commentary on the Gospel of Matthew* (Valley Forge: American Baptist Publication Society, 1886), p. 11.

47. R. Lenski, *Interpretation of St. Matthew's Gospel* (Columbus: Wartburg Press, 1943), p. 52.

48. Arndt and Gingrich, op. cit., p. 677.

Speaker in the Quotation

The observation of who is giving this quotation has also led to much discussion. First, it is clear that Matthew regarded its origin as being from God. He states that it was "spoken by the Lord through the prophet" (vs. 22). He, therefore, recognized that the sign given in Isaiah 7:14 was authored by God and delivered to Ahaz through the prophet. The preposition ὑπό introduces the direct agent with the passive verb, and διά the mediate agent. The actual speaker thus is *Yahweh* and the prophet is the medium or mouthpiece through which He speaks. "God is the *cause efficiens* (ὑπό), God's agent the *causa instrumentalis* (διά)."[49]

Secondly, there is the question of whether verse 22 is Matthew's editorial comment or whether it is actually a quotation of the angel's words to Joseph.[50] Significant influence could be given an interpretation of this passage if it is the angel of the Lord's statement.

In verse eighteen the angel confronts the alarmed Joseph in a dream to tell him of the genesis of Christ, relating both His conception and birth, but by the end of verse twenty-one has presented only the conception. He assures Joseph that Mary's pregnancy is of the Holy Spirit and, therefore, not of man. The actual birth of Jesus is not mentioned until verse twenty-five. To provide convincing evidence, the angel tells Joseph that she will give birth to a son who will save his people from their sins. Such a statement from God's angel carries great importance and implies the uniqueness of this child Jesus, who is born of the Holy Spirit. Quite obviously, the devout Jew knew that only God could save His people from their sins. The theological implications of the incarnation are the virgin birth of deity and, in particular, the deity of Jesus Christ. This declaration to Joseph is based on the angel's own word, and by the end of verse twenty-one Joseph has nothing to judge by but to wait

---

49. Lenski, op. cit., p. 53.

50. Lenski, ibid., seems to have been the first contemporary writer to point this out. Dr. Walvoord of Dallas Theological Seminary, in "Incarnation and the Son of God," *Bibliotheca Sacra* 117 (January, 1960): 6, agrees that the angel quoted this verse to Joseph as reassurance. Dr. Feinberg of Talbot Theological Seminary also agrees in "Virgin Birth in the Old Testament," *Bibliotheca Sacra* 117 (October, 1960): 324.

for the birth of the child and see whether it is a boy. Yet, because of
Mary's condition, an actual marriage is necessary immediately. Therefore, many maintain, the angel quotes the passage from Isaiah to
reassure Joseph, who immediately marries Mary (vs. 24). Therefore,
if verses twenty-two and twenty-three are the words of the angel, the
support of prophetic word to the angel's word would be very convincing to the troubled Joseph.[51]

Of course the implication of this viewpoint on the interpretation
of Matthew's quotation of Isaiah is very great. If the Lord's angel
declared this interpretation as a prediction of Mary's virgin-bearing
of Jesus, one would have great difficulty in denying the predictive
element. Needless to say, there are no quotation marks in the Greek
text; therefore, this argument cannot be substantially validated. It
does, however, make very good sense that the angel would offer
Joseph more assurance than his own word. The concept of the
angel's quoting Isaiah must remain in the area of possibility.

If the angel did not quote the verse to Joseph, on what basis does
Matthew use it? Many have said on the basis of the Septuagint
usage. However, there is one other very great possibility that is
often overlooked. Dr. Culver of Trinity Evangelical Divinity School
has pointed to the importance of Luke 2:24-27, 44-47.[52]

> In the prophets He taught them [His disciples] all things con-
> cerning Himself that must be fulfilled. . . . Then He opened their
> understanding that they might understand the Scriptures. . . .

What did He say? Did He teach them similarities to the Old Tes-
tament, or did He reveal Himself in its pages? If He did not reveal
Himself, why did His earliest followers claim that He did? Why did
Jesus Himself make this claim? After reading from the prophet Isaiah
(Luke 4:21), why did He declare, "This day is this prophecy ful-
filled"? When the Ethiopian eunuch (Acts 8:34) asked Philip, "Of
whom is the prophet speaking?" why did Philip begin "at the same
Scripture" and proclaim that it was Jesus? Was Philip wrong? Or,

---

51. Lenski, op. cit., pp. 51-53, maintains that the usage of the "fulfillment
formula" was taken from the angel's original statement, which Matthew then
applied to other sections as well.

52. Culver, op. cit., p. 91.

was Luke condoning conversions by using Scripture out of context? We come yet to the greater question for the purpose of this study: Where did Matthew get the idea that Isaiah 7:14 should be applied to Christ? Since he was one of the disciples who was taught by Jesus, is it not obvious that he got the "idea" from Jesus Christ Himself? Why would one of His own disciples make a contrary interpretation by "adding" a passage to the realm of prophetic fulfillment, when many other disciples were still living at the time and could have repudiated it?

Conclusion

Many have criticized conservative writers for accepting Matthew's statement at face value.[53] Yet look at the evidence. If Matthew followed the LXX in using παρθένος, he followed a source that represented the oldest available "interpretation" of Isaiah 7:14's rendering *'almah*. His contextual usage of ἵνα πληρωθῇ is almost certainly indicative of his understanding the Isaiah passage to contain a definitely predictive element. His recognition of the prophecy as coming from God shows that he felt his "interpretation" of it was also of God. It is also quite possible that verses 22-23 are not at all Matthew's narration but the recorded quotation of the angel's reassuring declaration to Joseph. Finally, it is obvious that Matthew was taught in the interpretation of messianic prophecy by Jesus Himself. Therefore, to say that Matthew made a mistake is to say that either the angel also made a mistake or Jesus Christ made one and passed it on to Matthew. Evangelical interpretation needs to take the stand of Ridderbos, who writes:

> So he, who was the Son of God, who was himself Immanuel ("God with us"), entered into the world of men under the name

----

53. For examples see: A. Gabelein, *The Gospel of Matthew* (Wheaton: Van Kampen, 1916), vol. I, p. 34. He refers to the critic's opinions as "ridiculous utterances . . . a denial of the integrity of the New Testament. . . ." H. Ironside, *Expository Notes on the Gospel of Matthew* (New York: Loizeaux Brothers, 1948), p. 14. He accepts Isaiah as predictive, without making any comment. A. Martin, *Isaiah: "The Salvation of Jehovah"* (Chicago: Moody Press, 1956), p. 39. He feels that Matthew's quote settles the matter of prediction and fulfillment. G. C. Morgan, op. cit., p. 48, states that Matthew provides "conclusive New Testament authority." J. Ryle, op. cit., p. 6. He also accepts Matthew's authority.

and protection of Joseph . . . but in all this He is Immanuel, "God with us," just as the prophet foretold.[54]

Having considered all the "evidence," Alexander concluded that it was overwhelmingly in favor of One who must be a God-man as Matthew said.[55] Matthew's recorded interpretation of the Isaiah passage as being predictive is of the highest probability of "correctness." It seems, therefore, that to reject it is to accept a much lesser possibility. It is interesting to note that Matthew closes his Gospel with Jesus' statement: "Lo, I am with you always"![56]

THE INTERPRETATION OF APOSTOLIC PREACHING AND WRITING

The inspired apostles had two factors to guide their interpretation of the Old Testament: (1) The explicit teaching of Jesus, (2) Implicit instruction and guidance of the Holy Spirit. Though there is no clear statement interpreting the virgin birth in Isaiah 7:14 other than Matthew's indication, there are many references to the virgin birth of the Messiah which are taken to be of Christ. Peter states that when the prophets wrote of Christ they did know that He should come, suffer, and afterward be glorified. He states that the only thing they were not certain about was the time of these events (as to when they should happen and for what duration).[57] According to our consideration of this passage in a previous section, we concluded that the prophets knew what they predicted. The implication of a "double-fulfillment" is that they really did not originally know they were speaking of Christ. Yet, the New Testament affirms often that they were so doing. Peter says of the prophets: ". . . they told of these days." To Cornelius (Acts 10:43) he said of Christ: "To Him all the prophets bear witness."

---

54. H. Ridderbos, *Matthew's Witness to Jesus Christ* (New York: Association Press, 1958), p. 21.

55. Alexander, op. cit., p. 120.

56. For an extensive bibliography on Matthew's use of the Old Testament, see R. H. Gundry, *The Use of the Old Testament in St. Matthew's Gospel: With Special Reference to the Messianic Hope* (Leiden: E. J. Brill, 1975), pp. 89ff. He argues that the reading in IQIs[a] can be pointed as *Kal* imperative קְרָא : "it [his name] shall be called" and that Matthew's use of καλέσουσιν may actually be following the Old Testament text rather than the LXX.

57. See I Peter 1:10-11.

Certainly the New Testament writers accepted Jesus' birth as a virgin birth bringing deity into the human race by means of the incarnation. "The Word was made flesh" (John 1:14); "God sending his own Son in the likeness of sinful flesh" (Rom. 8:3); "took upon himself the form of a servant and was made in the likeness of men" (Phil. 2:7); "great is the mystery of godliness: God was manifest in the flesh" (I Tim. 3:16). Certainly in the introduction of his letter to the Romans, Paul seems to presuppose a concept of the predicted birth of Christ in the gospel of God "which He promised beforehand through His prophets in the Holy Scriptures, concerning His Son, who was born of the seed of David according to the flesh, who was declared with power to be the Son of God. . . ."[58] Where in the writings of the prophets are we given a clearer picture of One born a man and yet who is God Himself, than in Isaiah's Immanuel, who through His birth is "God with us"?

---

58. Romans 1:2-4.

Chapter Five

SUMMARY

As a statesman Isaiah was one of the most prominent and erudite of the prophets of God. Residing in Jerusalem, his contacts with royalty were extensive, as was his influence in political matters. From the time of King Uzziah's death he had responded to the call of God to proclaim His truth to Judah. The latter half of the eighth century B.C. formed the backdrop of his life and work. In chapter seven of his book we have narrated the incident involving Ahaz and the threatened invasion from Syria and Ephraim. Ahaz's refusal to join their pact against Assyria caused them to attempt his overthrow, replacing him with one who would be more cooperative. To thwart their invasion Ahaz proposed that Judah form an alliance with Assyria. At that time Isaiah came forth to denounce the alliance and invoke the king's faith in God for protection. Having refused a confirmation of God's intention, Ahaz was forced to hear God's sign given by the prophet. At stake in the impending invasion was the kingdom of Judah, represented by the throne of David. To lose the throne meant the loss of the promise that it was to be an everlasting throne.

God's sign was the birth of Immanuel. Verse fourteen is the key to determining who He is to be. The prophet used the word *therefore* to connect his prediction with the foregoing reference to the king's unbelief. The sign comes from *Yahweh* Himself and is directed collectively to the "house of David," though spoken to Ahaz individually since he represented the Davidic line. Isaiah used the interjection "behold" to gain attention to the significance of *Yahweh's* sign.

The sign is that an *'almah* is pregnant and will bear a son, Immanuel. The definite article indicates that God (through the prophet) intends a definite, though unidentified, virgin, stressing her reality as a specific individual. The usage of *'almah* to designate the girl is most significant since it is always used in Scripture and non-biblical literature of the unmarried, young girls who have matured to the age of marriage. Though not the common word for "virgin," *'almah* always assures the intention of virginity. Its usage in legal marriage contracts for this purpose is most assuring of this meaning. The more common word for "virgin" is *bethūlah,* but it is, however, used sometimes of young widows who, of course, are no longer virgins. There is, therefore, every good reason to take this *'almah* to be an unmarried girl.

The time action in the verbal usage in this verse indicates that she is presently pregnant. The adjectival usage with the active participle denotes the present tense to the prophet's view. It is not uncommon for a prophet of God to speak in this manner. For example, throughout the second half of his book Isaiah speaks of the coming Babylonian captivity as already present and upon the people, and, at times, he even refers to it as though it were past. Thus, we see the certainty with which he considered God would bring these events to pass in history.

So certain is Isaiah of this birth that he speaks of it as though it were already happening. Why? First, because this was God's sign and therefore the prophet must have received this assurance from *Yahweh* since He gave it. Secondly, because it emphasizes an essential matter in the sign itself. The girl is a "virgin," and she also is pregnant (both at the same time). If a virgin were going to become pregnant, we would assume that she would marry first. But if she is already pregnant, as the verb seems to indicate, then we have to recognize here a miraculous birth, a virgin birth without a father.

What was this virgin's identity? Admittedly, without the New Testament no one would ever know for certain, for we are not told. Certainly no Old Testament woman fits this description. She is a real, definite individual. But who she is we are not told until Matthew said that she was Mary.

It must be stressed that the theological implications of the virgin birth and incarnation are tremendous. If Jesus is the sinless Saviour, incarnate in the flesh of humanity, we are compelled to see the necessity of His virgin birth whereby that holy thing in Mary is born of the Holy Spirit and not of man.

The name of the child was to be *Immanu-el,* "God with us." As all messianic names, it was intended as a description that characterized the person, rather than a title or name He used. Both the common expectation in those days of a divine Child who would come to rule and the description of His characteristics indicated His messianic nature to early interpreters. He was Himself what His name described—"God with us."

The contemporary significance of this sign to Ahaz came from the verses immediately following, which were both a warning and a promise to the Davidic line, represented in the person of Ahaz. He was warned to avoid alliance with Assyria since God would bring them deliverance Himself. He was assured that the throne of David would not be lost, for Immanuel must come to reign on it. However, he was also warned that Judah would see punishment as the result of their national unbelief, typified in himself.

The most important aspect in determining whether this prediction is actually messianic is a consideration of the whole context in which it appears. Chapter eight deals with coming problems with Assyria, which tried to overcome the land of Judah. Ahaz's alliance led to subjugation and vassalage. His unwillingness to heed God's warning and confirming sign showed his deep unfaithfulness and open rejection of God's help. Rather than confirming Judah's independence, he plunged her into irrevocable subjugation. However, God has not abandoned His people, for the land, though in the possession of the enemy, was still referred to as "thy land, O Immanuel."

In chapter nine Isaiah presents God's gift-child who is born unto His people as bearer of the government. He is connected to the birth of Immanuel in chapter seven. Here, though, we are given a much more complete description of who the virgin-born Immanuel is to be. His descriptive titles emphasize that He is *el gibbor,* the "mighty God" Himself. Thus, we see more clearly how it is that He is able to be born of a virgin. Even the accentuation of the passage supports this interpretation, so that we are confronted with an outright claim of deity for the virgin-born Messiah, who is to reign eternally in peace, subjugating the wicked.

In chapter eleven we are told that the line of David will be severed. So convinced is the prophet that again he describes it as having already happened. The tree of David is felled (a message of judgment), but a twig will yet sprout forth from the root stock of the tree and replenish it (a message of hope). The Messiah who is to come will be "delayed," for He must spring from the fallen tree that was tottering in Isaiah's day.

Is there any reason to confine this passage to a view of strict immediacy? The picture is very clear. A virgin-born Messiah will come to rule over the land in peace. These things He can do, for He is Himself God. Every indication of the total context points to a messianic prediction. There is significance in Isaiah's words to Ahaz. He is warned of possible doom if he does not heed God. He is confronted with the hope that God will not abandon His throne. Yet, he persists in sinful rejection. The Old Testament picture is very clear. The only details we lack are when this will happen and who is the "virgin."

The best views representing a dual-fulfillment view see the immediate "Immanuel" as the prophet's son or as Ahaz's son, Hezekiah. These views handle some of the problems of the interpretation of this passage and should be given thorough consideration by the objective investigator. There appear to be, however, some equally difficult problems caused by these views. Hezekiah cannot appropriately be fitted into the chronology to be yet unborn when the prophecy is delivered, and we have no indication later that Hezekiah was Isaiah's intended Immanuel. Also, he does not fit with the further descriptions in chapters nine through eleven.

The explanation of Immanuel as the prophet's son has a much better basis since he is actually referred to as a "sign." However, it is somewhat difficult to see how the birth of the prophet's son would be of comfort to Ahaz and cause him to forget the alliance with Assyria. Also, *Maher-shalal-hash-baz,* the son's name, is one of judgment on Judah and "Immanuel" is one of hope. In Isaiah 7:14 we are told that the girl will name the son "Immanuel," but in chapter eight God names the prophet's son and tells him to write it down. It is difficult to harmonize both accounts. Also, there is good reason to believe that Isaiah's wife had long been married to him and was the mother of his older son and, therefore, cannot be the *'almah* of chapter seven.

The earliest interpretation of this passage is possibly reflected in
Micah 5:3. This context gives the predicted birthplace of the
Messiah and refers to some definite woman who bears a son. Again
her pregnancy is seen as present and the child's birth as impending.
Since Micah was Isaiah's contemporary, this may well be a direct
quote from Isaiah. Though quite possible, it is difficult to demonstrate this conclusively.

However, the Septuagint's reference to the passage uses the Greek
word παρθένος, which means "virgin." Being very old, the LXX
probably reflects the common interpretation of these pre-Christian
days. There is, therefore, good evidence of early messianic interpretation of this passage, which indicates that the people of those days
apparently considered Isaiah to be making some sort of a virgin-birth
prediction.

Also, in the Greek material in the Qumran literature *parthenos* is
used to translate *'almah*. Also, much of the Hebrew literature, especially the commentaries, reflects a strong pre-Christian belief in a
virgin-born Messiah. Therefore, it is fallacious to contend that the
interpretation of Isaiah 7:14 as messianically applying to the birth of
Jesus is merely a Christian interpretation and invention, since there
is adequate pre-Christian evidence that such interpretation had a
Jewish origin. Various aspects of rabbinic teaching also support this
evidence. Both Palestinian and Alexandrian Jews took the passage
in Micah and the translation of the LXX as a messianic interpretation
of Isaiah 7:14. Also, many writers supported the interpretation of
the 7:14 passage as being a direct prediction of the Messiah's birth.

Historical attestation reveals that it was after the Christians interpreted Isaiah 7:14 as referring to Jesus that the Jewish writers
began to deny any messianic implication in the verse, and advocated
a contemporary fulfillment in Isaiah's day. This is the same viewpoint
that has been adopted by many writers during the past century. The
influence of the late nineteenth-century and early twentieth-century
critics caused many evangelicals to adopt a dual-fulfillment view of
this passage. However, the historical evidence gives very good indication that Isaiah meant the Immanuel prediction to refer to Christ,
since the earliest interpreters of the passage saw it as being messianic.

Finally, the New Testament view of this verse is reflected in

Matthew's quotation of it. The context is viewed in the sense of definite prophetic prediction, not merely a corresponding parallel. The usage of παρθένος indicates that the conception of Christ is viewed as a definite and complete (in one act) fulfillment of the prophet's prediction. With the Old Testament statement alone we know nothing of the mother's identity, except that she is to give birth to the Messiah. The question of identity is not answered until Matthew tells us that she is Mary and her son is Jesus.

This passage is quoted by Matthew for one of two reasons. Either to reassure his readers that the announcement of the angel to Joseph is in accord with the Old Testament prophetic picture, or it is a quotation of the angel's message to Joseph, in which he quotes this verse as a basis of authority invoking Joseph's trust in what he has told him. In either case, it must be admitted that the quotation of Isaiah 7:14 is for the purpose of confirming Jesus' birth as the direct plan of God's intentions.

Dr. Martin of Moody Bible Institute has well summarized the significance of this passage:

> Passages such as this test whether one really accepts the Bible as the Word of God or not. Liberal interpretation wallows in a quagmire of immediacy. . . . It must seek the complete explanation of the passage in the prophet's own day, and that in spite of the fact that the New Testament plainly declares otherwise.[1]

Where did Matthew get the idea that this passage in Isaiah was a prediction of Christ? The New Testament tells us he must have received it from one of two sources. Either the Holy Spirit directed him to it (John 14:20), or he was taught it directly by Jesus Christ (Luke 24:27, 44-45). To deny that Matthew has given us a proper interpretation of Isaiah is to deny that Jesus knew what He said of Himself as He instructed His disciples "in the prophets" concerning Himself. It is to deny His ability to "open their understanding that they might understand the scriptures."

The Old Testament context alone makes it clear that a child is to be born of a virgin and will come to rule on the throne of David,

---

1. Martin, *Isaiah: "The Salvation of Jehovah"* (Chicago: Moody Press, 1956), p. 39.

and His rule shall bring everlasting peace for He is "God with us." There is emphatically substantial evidence for interpreting the birth in Isaiah 7:14 as a virgin birth. There is good supporting evidence that the pre-Christian interpreters also saw this passage as a messianic virgin-birth prediction. Therefore, there is the highest degree of possibility that Matthew had every reason to assert the fulfillment of Isaiah's statement in the birth of Jesus Christ. Therefore, the New Testament provides an inspired interpretation to guide us. Therefore, we have the highest degree of probability that a direct, single-fulfillment of Isaiah's prediction is in the birth of Jesus. On this basis, it is a far less verifiable position to hold that the only fulfillment is in Isaiah's own day, or that there is a double fulfillment—then and again later in Jesus' time. An evaluation of the evidence reveals that Isaiah did in fact predict directly and in advance the birth of Jesus Christ by Mary, the virgin of Nazareth.

We need to heed the warning of Scripture: "O foolish men and slow to believe all that the prophets have spoken . . . neither recognizing Him nor the utterances of the prophets" (Luke 24:25; Acts 13:27). After the prophets had proclaimed His coming, Jesus showed His followers what they had foretold. May we not be so foolish as Ahaz to reject the sign God has given: "Behold, the virgin is pregnant and shall bear a son, and she shall call his name Immanuel." Isaiah's Immanuel is not merely a sign of his own times, but Jesus Christ, the sign of the ages.

BIBLIOGRAPHY

GENERAL REFERENCE

Allis, O. T. *The Old Testament: Its Claims and Its Critics.* Nutley: Presbyterian and Reformed, 1972.

Archer, G. *A Survey of Old Testament Introduction.* Chicago: Moody Press, 1964.

Berkhof, L. *Principles of Biblical Interpretation.* Grand Rapids: Baker, 1950.

Burrows, M. *An Outline of Biblical Theology.* Philadelphia: Westminster, 1946.

Davidson, A. B. *The Theology of the Old Testament.* New York: Scribner's Sons, 1904.

Driver, S. R. *An Introduction to the Literature of the Old Testament.* New York: Scribner's Sons, 1912.

Edersheim, A. *Prophecy and History in Relation to the Messiah.* Grand Rapids: Baker, 1955.

Eichrodt, W. *Theology of the Old Testament.* Vol I. Trans. J. Baker. Philadelphia: Westminster, 1961.

Eissfeldt, O. *The Old Testament: An Introduction.* New York: Harper & Row, 1965.

Girdlestone, R. *Old Testament Theology.* London: Longmans, Green & Co., 1909.

Gordon, C. *Introduction to Old Testament Times.* Ventor, N. J.: Ventor, 1953.

Harrison, R. K. *Introduction to the Old Testament.* Grand Rapids: Eerdmans, 1969.

Hengstenberg, E. *Christology of the Old Testament and a Commentary on Messianic Predictions.* 4 vols. Grand Rapids: Kregal, 1956.

Jacob, E. *Theology of the Old Testament.* Trans. A. Heathcote and P. Allcock. New York: Harper and Row, 1958.

Kitchen, K. *Ancient Orient and Old Testament.* Chicago: Inter-Varsity Press, 1966.

Klausner, J. *Messianic Idea in Israel.* New York: Macmillan, 1955.

Knight, G.A.F. *A Christian Theology of the Old Testament.* London: SCM Press, 1964.

Mickelsen, B. *Interpreting the Bible.* Grand Rapids: Eerdmans, 1963.

Noth, C. *History of Israel.* London: SCM Press, 1958.

Oehler, G. *Theology of the Old Testament.* New York: Funk and Wagnalls, 1883.

Orr, J. *The Problem of the Old Testament.* Boss Library. New York: Scribner's Sons, 1907.

Ramm, B. *Protestant Biblical Interpretation.* Boston: Wilde, 1954.

Schultz, H. *Old Testament Theology.* 2 vols. Edinburgh: T. & T. Clark, 1909.

Schultz, S. *The Old Testament Speaks.* New York: Harper & Row, 1960.

Snaith, N. *Distinctive Ideas of the Old Testament.* New York: Schocken, 1964.

Von Rad, G. *Old Testament Theology.* Vol. II. New York: Harper & Row, 1965.

Vos, G. *Biblical Theology.* Grand Rapids: Eerdmans, 1948.

Vriezen, T. *An Outline of Old Testament Theology.* Boston: Branford, 1958.

Young, E. *An Introduction to the Old Testament.* Grand Rapids: Eerdmans, 1954.

PROPHECY

Adams, J. *The Hebrew Prophets and Their Message for Today.* Edinburgh: T. & T. Clark, 1928.

Baron, D. *Rays of Messiah's Glory.* Grand Rapids: Zondervan, n.d.

Beecher, W. J. *The Prophets and the Promise.* Grand Rapids: Baker, reprint of 1909 ed.

Briggs, C. *Messianic Prophecy.* New York: Scribner's Sons, 1892.

Carroll, B. *The Prophets of the Assyrian Period.* Nashville: Broadman, 1948.

Cooper, D. *Messiah: His Redemptive Career.* Los Angeles: Biblical Research Society, 1935.

Culver, R. "Were the Old Testament Prophecies Really Prophetic?" in *Can I Trust My Bible?* Chicago: Moody Press, 1963.

Davidson, A. B. *Old Testament Prophecy.* Edinburgh: T. & T. Clark, 1903.

Dewart, E. *Jesus the Messiah in Prophecy and Fulfillment.* Cincinnati: Cranston & Stowe, 1891.

Ellison, H. L. *Men Spake from God.* Grand Rapids: Eerdmans, 1952.

Fohrer, G. *Die Propheten des Alten Testaments.* 7 vols. Gütersloher: Gerd Mohn, 1974.

Freeman, H. *An Introduction to the Old Testament Prophets.* Chicago: Moody Press, 1968.

Greenstone, J. *The Messianic Idea in Jewish History.* Philadelphia: Jewish Publication Society of America, 1943.

Hughes, P. E. *Interpreting Prophecy.* Grand Rapids: Eerdmans, 1976.

Jelf, G. *Messiah Cometh.* London: Innes & Co., 1899.

Kirkpatrick, A. *The Doctrine of the Prophets.* Grand Rapids: Zondervan, 1958.

Kittel, R. *Great Men and Movements in Israel.* New York: Macmillan, 1929.

Klausner, J. *The Messianic Idea in Israel.* Trans. W. Stinespring. New York: Macmillan, 1955.

Klingerman, A. *Messianic Prophecy in the Old Testament.* Grand Rapids: Zondervan, 1958.

Kraeling, E. *The Prophets.* New York: Rand McNally, 1969.

Mowinckel, S. *He That Cometh.* New York: Abingdon, 1954.

Reich, M. *The Messianic Hope of Israel.* Chicago: Moody Press, 1945.

Reihm, E. *Messianic Prophecy.* Edinburgh: T. & T. Clark, 1900.

Silver, A. *A History of Messianic Speculation in Israel.* New York: Macmillan, 1927.

Smith, W. R. *The Prophets of Israel.* New York: Appleton and Co., 1882.

Studies in Prophecy: A Collection of Twelve Papers. Leiden: E. J. Brill, 1974.

Thompson, W. *The Great Argument or Jesus in the Old Testament.* New York: Harper & Brothers, 1884.

Von Rad, G. *The Message of the Prophets.* New York: Harper & Row, 1965.

Winward, S. *A Guide to the Prophets.* Richmond: John Knox Press, 1969.

Young, E. *My Servants the Prophets.* Grand Rapids: Eerdmans, 1947.

WRITINGS OF ISAIAH

Aberly, J. "The Book of Isaiah," in H. Alleman and E. Flack, ed., *Old Testament Commentary.* Philadelphia: Fortress Press, 1948.

Alexander, J. A. *The Earlier Prophecies of Isaiah.* New York and London: Wiley & Putnam, 1846; reprinted by Zondervan, 1970.

Allis, O. T. *The Unity of Isaiah.* Philadelphia: Presbyterian and Reformed, 1950.

Archer, G. L. "Isaiah," in C. Pfeiffer and E. Harrison. *The Wycliffe Bible Commentary.* Chicago: Moody Press, 1962.

Barnes, A. *Notes on the Old Testament: Isaiah.* Grand Rapids: Baker, 1964.

Bentzen, A. *Jesaja.* Copenhagen: Forlag, 1944.

Bertram, R., and A. Tucker. *A Homiletical Commentary on the Prophecies of Isaiah.* New York: Funk and Wagnalls, n.d.

Birks, T. *Commentary on the Book of Isaiah.* London: Church of England Book Society, 1878.

Blank, S. H. *Prophetic Faith in Isaiah.* New York: Harper & Row, 1958.

Boutflower, C. *The Book of Isaiah.* London: Society for Promotion of Christian Knowledge, 1930.

Bruno, D. A. *Jesaja.* Stockholm: Almquist & Wiksell, 1953.

Calvin, J. *Commentary on the Book of the Prophet Isaiah.* Grand Rapids: Eerdmans, 1953 ed.

Caspari, C. *Jesajanische Studien.* Leipzig: Verlag Von Fritzsche, 1843.

Cheyne, T. K. *The Prophecies of Isaiah.* 2 vols. New York: Whittaker, 1888.

Clark, A. *The Holy Bible With a Commentary and Critical Notes: Old Testament.* Vol. IV. New York: Abingdon-Cokesbury, 1823.

Cook, F. C. *The Holy Bible With Explanatory and Critical Commentary.* Vol. V. New York: Scribner's Sons, 1886.

Copass, B. A. *Isaiah, Prince of the Old Testament Prophets.* Nashville: Broadman Press, 1944.

Cowles, H. *Isaiah: With Notes.* New York: Appleton and Co., 1869.

De Leeuw, V. *De Ebed Jahweh-Profetieen.* Leuven: Van Gorcum 1956.

Delitzsch, F. *Biblical Commentary on the Old Testament: Isaiah.* Vol. I. Grand Rapids: Eerdmans, 1949.

Dillmann, A. *Das Prophet Jesaia.* Leipzig: Von Hirzel, 1890.

Doerne, F. *Jesaja der König unter den Propheten.* Leipzig: Berlag von Friedrich Jahja, 1904.

Dreschler, M. *Der Prophet Jesaja.* Stuttgart: Gustav Schlawitz, 1849.

Driver, S. R. *Isaiah: His Life and Time.* London: Nisbet and Company, 1888.

Duhm, B. *Das Buch Jesaia.* Gottingen, 1922.

Erdman, C. R. *The Book of Isaiah.* New York: Revell, 1954.

Exell, J. *The Biblical Illustrator: Isaiah.* Vol. I. New York: Revell, n.d.

Fisher, J. *Das Buch Isaias.* 2 vols. Bonn: Peter Hanstein, 1937.

Fitch, W. "Isaiah," in F. Davidson, *The New Bible Commentary.* Grand Rapids: Eerdmans, 1954.

Gaebelein, A. *The Annotated Bible.* Vol XIV. Wheaton: Van Kampen, 1921.

Gesenius, W. *Commentar uber den Jesaia.* Leipzig: Wilhelm Vogel, 1821.

Glazebrook, M. *Studies in the Book of Isaiah.* Oxford: Clarendon Press, 1910.

Gordon, A. R. *The Faith of Isaiah.* London: James Clark & Co., 1919.

Gray, G. *The Book of Isaiah.* Vol. I, International Critical Commentary. New York: Scribner's Sons, 1912.

Henry, M. *Commentary on the Whole Bible.* Vol. IV. New York: Revell, n.d.

Interpreter's Bible. Vol. V. New York: Abingdon, 1956.

Jefferson, C. *Cardinal Ideas in Isaiah.* New York: Macmillan, 1925.

Jennings, F. *Studies in Isaiah.* New York: Loizeau Brothers, 1950.

Kaiser, O. *Isaiah 1–12.* Old Testament Library. Philadelphia: Westminster, 1972.

Keith, A. *Isaiah As It Is.* Edinburgh: Whyte & Co., 1850.

Kelly, W. *An Exposition of the Book of Isaiah.* London: Hammond, 1947.

Kissane, E. *The Book of Isaiah.* 2 vols. Dublin: Browne & Nolan, 1941.

König, E. *Das Buch Jesaja.* Gütersloh: Bertelsmann, 1926.

Lack, R. *La Symbolique du Livre d'Isaïe.* Rome: Pontifical Biblical Institute, 1973.

Leslie, E. A. *Isaiah.* New York: Abingdon, 1963.

Lindbolm, S. *A Study of the Immanuel Section of Isaiah.* Lund, 1958.

Lowth, R. *Isaiah.* Boston: Buckingham, 1815.

MacClaren, A. *Expositions of Holy Scripture: Isaiah Chapters I–XLVIII.* New York: Hodder Stoughton, 1906.

Martin, A. *Isaiah: "The Salvation of Jehovah."* Chicago: Moody Press, 1956.

Mauchline, J. *Isaiah 1–39.* New York: Macmillan, 1962.

Morgan, G. C. *The Prophecy of Isaiah.* Vol. I, *Analysed Bible.* London: Hodder & Stoughton, 1910.

Muckle, J. *Isaiah 1–39.* London: Epworth, 1960.

Nagelsbach, C. *The Prophet Isaiah.* J. Lange, ed., *A Commentary on the Holy Scriptures.* New York: Scribner's Sons, 1906.

Orelli, C. *The Prophecies of Isaiah.* Edinburgh: T. & T. Clark, 1895.

Plumtre, E. H. "Isaiah," in C. Ellicott, ed., *A Bible Commentary For English Readers.* Vol. IV. New York: Cassell and Co., n.d.

Price, R. "Isaiah," in *Beacon Bible Commentary.* Vol. IV. Kansas City: Beacon Hill, 1966.

Raven, J. J. *Emmanuel.* London: Longmans, Green, Reader, and Dyer, 1872.

Robinson, G. L. *The Book of Isaiah.* Grand Rapids: Baker, 1964.

Rowlinson, G. *Isaiah.* Vol. I, H. Spence and J. Exell, ed., *The*

Pulpit Commentary. London and New York: Funk and Wagnalls, 1913.

Schilling, P. *Isaiah Speaks.* New York: Crowell, 1958.

Simeon, C. *Expository Outlines on the Whole Bible: Isaiah.* London: Bolm, 1847.

Simpson, A. B. *Isaiah.* Harrisburg, Pa.: Christian Publications, n.d.

Skinner, J. *The Book of the Prophet Isaiah I–XXXIX.* Cambridge Series. Cambridge: University Press, 1900.

Smith, G. A. *The Book of Isaiah.* Vol. I. New York: Harper & Brothers, 1927.

Vine, W. E. *Isaiah: Prophecies, Promises, Warnings.* London: Oliphants, 1953.

Ward, J. *Amos and Isaiah.* Nashville: Abingdon, 1969.

Williams, G. *The Student's Commentary on the Holy Scriptures.* Grand Rapids: Kregal, 1953.

Wordsworth, W. A. *En-Roeh: The Prophecies of Isaiah the Seer.* Edinburgh: T. & T. Clark, 1939.

Young, E. J. *Studies in Isaiah.* Grand Rapids: Eerdmans, 1954.

————. *The Book of Isaiah.* 3 vols. New International Commentary Series. Grand Rapids: Eerdmans, 1965–1972.

————. *Who Wrote Isaiah?* Pathway Series. Grand Rapids: Eerdmans, 1958.

MATTHEW'S GOSPEL

Argyle, A. *The Gospel According to Matthew.* Cambridge Bible Commentary Series. Cambridge: University Press, 1963.

Barnes, A. *Notes on the New Testament: Matthew and Mark.* Grand Rapids: Baker, 1964.

Bornkamm, G., G. Barth, H. J. Held. *Tradition and Interpretation in Matthew.* Philadelphia: Westminster, 1963.

Broadus, J. *Commentary on the Gospel of Matthew.* American Commentary Series. Valley Forge, Pa.: American Baptist Publication Society, 1886.

Cox, G. E. *The Gospel According to St. Matthew.* Torch Series. London: SCM Press, 1956.

Earle, R. "Matthew," in the *Wesleyan Bible Commentary*. Grand Rapids: Eerdmans, 1964.

Filson, J. *A Commentary on the Gospel According to St. Matthew*. Harper Series. New York: Harper & Row, 1959.

Gaebelein, A. C. *The Gospel of Matthew*. Vol. I. Wheaton: Van Kampen, 1916.

Hamilton, W. *Modern Reader's Guide to Matthew and Luke*. New York: Association Press, 1959.

Hendriksen, W. *A Commentary on the Gospel of Matthew*. Grand Rapids: Baker, 1972.

Hindson, E. "Gospel According to Matthew," in J. Falwell, E. Hindson, and W. Kroll, eds., *Liberty Bible Commentary*. Lynchburg: Liberty Press, 1978.

Ironside, H. *Expository Notes on the Gospel of Matthew*. New York: Loizeaux Brothers, 1948.

Kent, H., Jr. "Matthew," in C. Pfeiffer and E. Harrison, ed., *Wycliffe Bible Commentary*. Chicago: Moody Press, 1962.

Lenski, R. *Interpretation of St. Matthew's Gospel*. Columbus, Ohio: Wartburg Press, 1943.

MacClaren, A. *Expositions of the Holy Scripture: Matthew I–VIII*. New York: Hodder and Stoughton, 1906.

Ridderbos, H. N. *Matthew's Witness to Jesus Christ*. New York: Association Press, 1958.

Rogers, E. W. *Jesus the Christ: A Study of Matthew's Gospel*. London: Pickering and Inglis, 1962.

Ryle, J. C. *Expository Thoughts on the Gospels: Matthew-Luke*. Grand Rapids: Zondervan, n.d.

Stonehouse, N. B. *The Witness of Matthew and Mark to Christ*. London: Lutterworth, 1944.

Tasker, R. V. G. *Gospel According to St. Matthew*. Tyndale Commentary Series. Grand Rapids: Eerdmans, 1961.

Walvoord, J. *Matthew: Thy Kingdom Come*. Chicago: Moody Press, 1974.

VIRGIN BIRTH

Birch, W. G. *Veritas and Virgin*. Berne, Ind.: Berne Witness Inc., 1960.

Bonsall, H. *The Person of Christ*. London: Christian Literature Crusade, 1967.

Boslooper, T. D. *The Virgin Birth*. Philadelphia: Westminster, 1962.

Brown, H. H. *When Jesus Comes*. Grand Rapids: Eerdmans, 1963.

Buksbazen, V. *Miriam, The Virgin of Nazareth*. Philadelphia: Spearhead Press, 1963.

Cullmann, O. *The Christology of the New Testament*. Philadelphia: Westminster, 1959.

Dayton, W. "Virgin Birth," in M. Tenney, ed. *Zondervan Pictorial Encyclopedia of the Bible*. Grand Rapids: Zondervan, 1975.

Gromacki, R. *The Virgin Birth: Doctrine of Deity*. New York: Thomas Nelson, 1974.

Hanke, H. A. *The Validity of the Virgin Birth*. Grand Rapids: Zondervan, 1963.

Hoben, A. *The Virgin Birth*. Chicago: University of Chicago Press, 1903.

Kasper, W. *Jesus the Christ*. New York: Paulist Press, 1976.

Lawlor, G. *Almah . . . Virgin or Young Woman?* Des Plains, Ill.: Regular Baptist Press, 1973.

Machen, J. G. *The Virgin Birth of Christ*. New York: Harper and Brothers, 1930.

McDonald, H. D. *Jesus—Human and Divine*. Grand Rapids: Zondervan, 1968.

Murray, J. "Incarnation," in *Wycliffe Bible Encyclopedia*. Chicago: Moody Press, 1975.

Northrup, B. *The Use of Almah in Isaiah 7:14*. Unpublished Masters's Thesis. Dallas Theological Seminary, 1955.

Palmer, J. *The Virgin Birth*. New York: Macmillan, 1924.

Sadler, M. *Emmanuel*. London: Bell & Daldy, 1867.

Skard, B. *The Incarnation*. Trans. H. Jorgenson. Minneapolis: Augsburg, 1960.

Smith, W. *The Supernaturalness of Christ*. Boston: W. A. Wilde Co., 1944.

Taylor, V. *The Historical Evidence for the Virgin Birth*. Oxford: Clarendon Press, 1920.

Walker, W. *The Spirit and the Incarnation*. Edinburgh: T. & T. Clark, 1899.

Periodical Articles

Barr, J. "The Word Became Flesh." *Interpretation* X. Richmond (January, 1956): 16-23.

Bird, J. "Who Is the Boy in Isaiah vii.16?" *Catholic Biblical Quarterly* VI. Washington, D.C. (1944): 433-43.

Blank, S "Immanuel and Which Isaiah?" *Journal of Near Eastern Studies* XIII. Chicago (1954): 83-86.

Bratcher, T. "A Study of Isaiah vii.14." *Bible Translator* IX. London (1958): 97-126.

Brown, R. "Problem of the Virginal Conception of Jesus." *Theological Studies* XXXIII (1972): 3-34.

Carnell, E. "Virgin Birth of Christ." *Christianity Today* IV. Washington, D.C. (December 7, 1959): 9-10.

Clark, A. "The Virgin Birth: A Theological Reappraisal." *Theological Studies* XXIV (1973): 576-93.

Coppens, A. *"La Prophetie de le 'Almah." Ephemrides Theologicae Louvenienes* XXVIII (1952): 648-78.

Culver, R. "The Old Testament as Messianic Prophecy." *Bulletin of the Evangelical Theological Society* VII. Wheaton (Summer, 1964): 91-97.

De Santo, C. "Theological Key to the Gospel of John." *Evangelical Quarterly* XXXIV. London (April, 1964).

Feinberg, C. "Virgin Birth in the Old Testament." *Bibliotheca Sacra* 117. Dallas (October, 1960): 313-24.

──────. "Virgin Birth in the Old Testament and Isaiah 7:14." *Bibliotheca Sacra* 119. Dallas (July, 1962): 251-58.

Flynn, L. "What's So Unusual About the Birth of Christ?" *Christian Life* XXIII. Chicago (December, 1961): 22-24.

Gordon, C. *"Almah* in Isaiah 7:14." *Journal of Bible and Religion* XXI. Philadelphia (1953): 106.

Gottwald, G. "Immanuel as the Prophet's Son." *Vetus Testamentum* VIII. Leiden (1958): 36-47.

Hammershaimb, H. "The Immanuel Sign." *Studia Theologicae* III (1950–51): 124-42.

Heinitz, K. "Pannenberg: Theology (From Below) and the Virgin Birth." *Lutheran Quarterly* XXVIII (1976): 173-82.

Hindson, E. "Development of the Interpretation of Isaiah 7:14." *Grace Journal* X, 2 (Spring, 1969): 19-25.

─────. "Isaiah's Immanuel." *Grace Journal* X, 3 (Fall, 1969): 3-15.

Hinson, W. "Virgin Birth: A Fact." *Evangelical Christian* (December, 1954): 3-5.

Hitt, R. "Who Is Jesus Christ?" *Eternity* XIV. Philadelphia (February, 1963): 8.

Howard T. "God Before Birth: The Imagery Matters." *Christianity Today* XXI (December 17, 1976): 10-13.

Hume, C. "Virgin Birth: Divers Approaches." *Church Quarterly Review* 168 (1967): 462-66.

Irwin, J. "That Troublesome Almah and Other Matters." *Review and Expositor* L. Louisville (1953): 337-60.

Johnson, S. "Genesis of Jesus." *Bibliotheca Sacra* 122. Dallas (October, 1965): 331-42.

Kelly, H. "Christ, Born of a Virgin." *United Evangelical Action* XV. Wheaton (December 15, 1957): 451-52.

Kissane, W. "Butter and Honey Shall He Eat." *Bible Lovers.* (1957): 169-73.

Kraeling, E. "The Immanuel Prophecy." *Journal of Biblical Literature* L. Philadelphia (1931): 277-97.

Lust, J. "Immanuel Figure: A Charismatic Judge-Leader (Isaiah 7:10-17)." *Ephremerides Theologicae Lovanienses* XLIII (1971): 464-70.

Moody, D. "Isaiah 7:14 in the RSV." *Review and Expositor* 50 (1953): 61-68.

Mueller, W. "A Virgin Shall Conceive." *Evangelical Quarterly* XXXII. London (October, 1960): 203-07.

Payne, B. "So-Called Fulfillment in Messianic Psalms." *Printed Papers of the Evangelical Theological Society*. Chicago (1953): 62-72.

Piper, O. "Virgin Birth: The Meaning of the Gospel Accounts." *Interpretation* XVIII. Richmond (April, 1964): 131-48.

Porubean, A. "The Word '*ot* in Isaiah 7:14." *Catholic Biblical Quarterly* XXII. Washington, D.C. (1960): 144-59.

Ramm, B. "God Tented Among Us." *His* XXV. Chicago (December, 1964): 1-4.

Rehm, G. "Das Wort *'almah* in Is. VII." *Biblische Zeitschrift* (1964): 89-101.

Rice, G. "The Genre of Isaiah 7:15-17." *Journal of Biblical Literature* 96 (1977): 363-69.

Richardson, H. "Theological Reflections on the Virgin Birth." *Marian Studies* XXIV (1973): 66-82.

Robinson, W. "A Re-Study of the Virgin Birth of Christ." *Evangelical Quarterly* XXXVII. London (October, 1965): 198-211.

Rowley, G. "Comparison and Contrast." *Interpretation* XVI. Richmond (July, 1962): 292-304.

Runia, K. "Conceived by the Holy Spirit, Born of the Virgin Mary." *Christianity Today* XIX (December 6, 1974): 5-7.

Saliba, J. "The Virgin Birth in Anthropological Literature: A Critical Assessment." *Theological Studies* XXXVI (1975): 428-54.

Sauer, A. "Problems of Messianic Interpretation." *Concordia Theological Monthly* XXV. St. Louis (October, 1964): 566-74.

Schulz, H. *"Alma" Biblische Zeitschrift* (1935–36): 229-41.

Scullion, J. "Approach to the Understanding of Isaiah 7:10-17." *Journal of Biblical Literature* 87, (1968): 228-300.

Taylor, J. "Born of a Virgin." *Christianity Today* IX. Washington, D.C. (December 18, 1964): 9-10.

Vawter, W. "The Ugaritic Use of *glmt.*" *Catholic Biblical Quarterly* XXII. Washington, D.C. (1952): 318-22.

Walvoord, J. "Incarnation of the Son of God." *Bibliotheca Sacra* 117. Dallas (January, 1960): 3-12.

Wilson, R. D. "The Meaning of Alma (A.V. 'Virgin') in Isaiah VII. 14." *Princeton Theological Review* 24 (1926).

Wolf, H. "Solution to the Immanuel Prophecy in Isaiah 7:14." *Journal of Biblical Literature* 91 (1972): 449-56.